THE DNA
of a Game Warden

WASHINGTON FISH AND WILDLIFE CAPTAIN BUD HOLSTE

ISBN: 9798385767021

Printed in the United States of America

This book is dedicated to John Adams, an Ohio game protector, for helping me get hired with the Ohio Division of Wildlife in 1965; to Bob Ford, a good friend who kept telling me to move west and to apply for a wildlife agent position with the Washington Game Department; to Walter Neubrech, chief of the Game Department Enforcement Division, for taking a chance on hiring me in 1971; and also in memory of my friend Terry Hoffer, a Washington wildlife agent who was killed in the line of duty in 1984.

CONTENTS

INTRODUCTION

The oldest images of hunting are etched in crude and strange drawings on the walls of caves and upon the face of prominent rock outcroppings. Mankind and our ancestors were hunter-gatherers using stones, clubs, and spears to kill wild animals for food and to use their skins and feathers for clothing and canoes.

When European kings ruled over land and people, they owned the land and wildlife. After the American colonies declared their independence, things changed. Early in American history, the Supreme Court ruled that wildlife in this country belonged to all the people, which led to public hunting and fishing.

Wildlife populations were so abundant, regulations and limits didn't seem necessary. Since no one person owned the wildlife, it was killed for commercial purposes to feed the early settlers, miners, and railroad workers as the West was settled. The hides, meat, and feathers were sold in an unregulated marketplace.

The passenger pigeon became extinct, and the great bison herds were almost wiped out as well. Americans became concerned and started to restore and conserve fish and wildlife. Those early Americans, almost without exception, were hunters.

Fish and wildlife agencies were formed; rules and regulations with time, place, limits, and manner to harvest were enacted; and officers were paid and commissioned to enforce those regulations. Those early officers were called game wardens.

The word game warden is the generic term for a group of wildlife enforcement officers, be they game protectors, wildlife agents, conservation officers, wildlife rangers or fish and wildlife protectors. I was one of those game wardens for thirty-one and a half years, from January 11, 1965, until retiring in June 30, 1996. The game law violator is a thief:

they steal your opportunity to harvest a trophy or to put meat in the freezer. Fishing, hunting or killing wildlife during the closed season, at night, or taking in excess of the daily limit is called poaching. Many people wouldn't turn in a family member or friend; however, a few would and did. I thanked them and kept their identity a secret unless they had to testify to convict the violator.

When I attended club meetings, people would tell me they knew poachers but didn't want to identify them. I would tell them that didn't matter to me as I got paid if I caught them or didn't catch them. I didn't get paid for the number of arrests I made. However, their poacher friend was stealing their chance and mine to catch a fish or shoot a deer during the season.

The events and stories told here are true. They are my thoughts and reflections at the time with hopes of giving some young person more respect for wildlife and to stimulate the mind of another officer on ways to solve a wildlife crime.

Some of the events I thought were humorous and, to some extent, entertaining. Most poachers are not professional speakers, so I apologize for not always being politically correct or not using the most proper form of the English language. I should have paid more attention to my English teacher in high school. I never thought I would someday want to write a book. Some names have been changed to protect their identity, except for those deserving credit for their contributions to my story.

I developed from a boy to a man to a poacher hunter to a career wildlife enforcement officer. My poaching occurred in the early years of my life, on non-threatened or endangered species that reproduced rapidly. I do not condone getting an education this way but remembering those methods, along with a lot of patience, helped me catch a lot of poachers. Being in the right place, at the right time, helped a lot too.

Maybe catching poachers and protecting the fish and wildlife and the natural resources of our country for thirty-one and a half years helped balance the bad and good parts of my life and career. I worked long hours and had fun doing it. If a person doesn't enjoy doing the day-to-day tasks of their profession, it is time to make a change. A person chooses a career path but makes choices on how to succeed.

I tried to always treat other coworkers and violators as I would like to be treated. One woman violator was mad about getting a ticket and was chipping her teeth and cussing while I was writing her a ticket and told me I was mean. Finally, very politely, I looked at her and said, "But I'm fair—I'm mean to everybody." She gave me a dirty look and shut up.

I caught a lot of poachers over the years and had a good conviction rate. Some of them even thanked me for treating them fair and vowed never to poach again. Some never learned, and I caught them more than once. Most people obey the laws when standing in front of a uniformed officer, but when I worked undercover, their bad habits would show through.

I enjoyed all phases of wildlife protection and enjoyed working with and on wildlife as much as working with the people who did it for recreation. Doing surveys, banding, tagging, or just relocating critters was fun for me. Some officers would complain about having to take driver's training, defensive tactics, and firearms qualification. I would tell them to quit complaining, the state provided their uniforms, their vehicle, and their gas; and they were getting paid to do it, enjoy it. With years of practice, I became proficient with firearms to dispatch injured wildlife, to protect my life, other officers, and the public. I was a firearms instructor and trained other officers for the department and even impressed a few of them with some trick shooting. I was blessed and very humble to have the natural ability to shoot rifles, shotguns, pistols, and a bow and arrows with a great deal of accuracy. Hitting objects out of the air, running and at great distances, became easy for me.

Most of my firearms were far more accurate than what I could squeeze out of them in my excited state of mind upon seeing a true trophy in front of me. I have been blessed to be able to hunt small game in Illinois and Ohio and big game in Alaska, Canada, Idaho, Michigan, Montana, Pennsylvania, Utah, West Virginia, Wyoming, and Washington. I was able to eat the meat from antelopes, black and brown bears, caribous, deer, elk, mountain goats, moose, and Dall sheep. The money I spent on a hunting license in those states helped protect the wildlife for future hunters.

I was able to survive rafting white water on class 5 rapids on the Colorado River in the Grand Canyon and other rivers in Canada, Idaho, Oregon, Washington, and South America. Now that I am retired, I hunt in different habitats and different species of game and fowl, with more emphasis on the hunt than on food for the freezer. I didn't always have to kill wildlife to enjoy hunting as I often took my favorite rifle for long walks and only received exercise for my efforts.

When I attended club meetings, the sportsmen would always try to find out the best place to go hunting for a deer or to find the best place to catch some fish. They would ask me, "Where was a good place to shoot a deer?" I would tell them, "Right behind the ear." If they asked, "Where was a good place to catch a fish?" and I knew the person, I would stick my finger in the corner of my mouth and say, "Right here."

I enjoy watching wildlife, fishing, and hunting; and my career allowed me many opportunities to do that. I tried to develop the same interest in my family, friends, and others. My instincts and, on a couple occasions, a compass always brought me back to my truck, so I never had to spend a cold night in the woods walking around a tree to keep warm.

Be alert to danger signals, stay safe, keep your powder dry, shoot straight, and maybe someday I'll see you in the field and show you my secret spot to shoot a deer. It was an honor, and I was very proud and humble to be allowed to be a game warden.

THE EARLY YEARS

My older sister couldn't say "baby brother" after I was born and would call me "baby buddy." So I answered to the name of Bud ever since I was old enough to remember. I sign my checks, legal documents, and tickets with Harold Holste so they don't get thrown out of court on a technicality.

When I was four years old, my family moved from the big city of Chicago to a farm in the country, near the little town of Altamont, Illinois, near the town where I was born. I always loved looking for wildlife when riding in the car with family and friends. I would never go to sleep at night, riding home from church, town, or a friend's birthday party, afraid I would miss seeing a rabbit run across the road in front of the car.

When we were young, my sisters and I would listen to the Lone Ranger and Tonto on the radio and ride our broom ponies all day and play cowboys and Indians. I always played the good guy. I got my first cap guns for Christmas and lost them the same night. I put on my double set of holsters and shiny noisemakers and was king of the cowboys.

That night, my uncle and dad took me out to the barn to look at the cows and a new calf. They put me down in the feed stall, and being a small lad, I was afraid of those big ugly cows. My gun belt slipped off my hips as I jumped out of the manger and was lost until my dad found it the next morning.

I got my first BB gun, a single-shot Daisy air rifle, when I was five or six years old. The gun had to be pumped, by breaking it in half, each time I wanted to shoot it. I was pretty good with it and would use one BB for small birds and two BBs for pigeons. I shot sparrows, pigeons, starlings, blackbirds, and sometimes when my cousin Lawrence came over with his BB gun, we would shoot the old bull in the butt.

I didn't think the BB gun had enough power to kill pigeons, so I let my younger sister, Joyce, shoot me with it. Kids, don't ever try this at home. I had my winter wool coat on and stood with my back to her by the horse barn. She stood across the driveway, about fifty feet away, and aimed for the center of my back. The BB went low and hit me in the back of my left knee, in the soft spot. I jumped around a little because it hurt like heck! I never did that again.

When I was eight, I got a Daisy Red Ryder lever action that held a half a pack of BBs in the tube on the barrel. It was more accurate and shot harder than the single shot. I got smarter as I got older, so when it came to testing the power of the BB, I shot it into a piece of wood to see which BB would go in the deepest. A pack of BBs, a cardboard tube about the size of a 12-gauge shotshell, cost a nickel and would last over a month.

I never did count how many there were in a pack, but there were lots when I spilled them on the floor and had to pick them up. I was deadly on starlings that ate our strawberries and sat on the electric line near their nest in the big maple trees in the yard. Joyce and I would clean the sparrows out of the hen house at night; she held the flashlight while I shot them.

Lawrence was in 4-H. They had a pest hunt each winter, so we would go into my Uncle Clarence's hen house at night and shoot fifty to one hundred sparrows. We had to cut the feet off the birds and turn them in to collect points. Sparrows counted ten points, starlings twenty-five, pigeons fifty, and a crow was worth a hundred points.

My grampa had a model 62, Winchester pump-action .22 rimfire rifle with a hammer that would only shoot shorts. That style of rifle was mostly used in shooting galleries. There were .22 shorts, long, and long-rifle cartridges back in the old days. Grampa sanded the rust off the rifle with sandpaper, and it looked like stainless steel because all the bluing had been sanded off.

My BB gun was just as big as his little rifle. My grampa told me, so I guess it was true that the rifle would put a bullet dead center in the target every time. Especially if he would shoot at the target and then go draw a circle around the bullet hole!

Grampa always kept the rifle loaded on the back porch and told me not to point it at anything I didn't want to kill because once you pull the trigger, you could never call that bullet back. I guess the kids back in those days had more sense and didn't play cops and robbers with real guns. Grampa would carry the .22 rifle along to shoot bullfrogs and turtles when we went fishing in his pond.

There were lots of nonpoisonous water moccasin snakes around his pond, and they would always scare the heck out of me when they took off through the weeds at my feet. I would have nightmares about snakes when I was a small child. They were all shapes and sizes and would walk on their tails and chase me wherever I went. I couldn't get away from them. I guess they made me the good hunter that I am today because I still look at the ground to see that I don't step on snakes or sticks when I am walking in the outdoors.

When I was eleven or twelve, Grampa said I could take his rifle out to the orchard by myself and shoot starlings, blackbirds, and sparrows that were eating his cherries. I was so excited I went out and didn't ask him how to load or unload the rifle. I didn't shoot anything and didn't know how to get the bullet out of the chamber, so I went behind the barn, where no one could see me, and experimented until I knew how to operate it. So much for hunter education. Some say I got my education out behind the barn.

Mom and Dad got divorced in 1954 when I was thirteen, and I spent a lot of time with Grampa and the little rifle. I went target shooting at the edge of town with some friends who had a rifle and .410 shotgun. We were unsupervised, and someone shot a dove out of season, thus was the start of my poaching career.

We decided to eat the dove, so we picked the feathers off it and washed it in the creek and built a small fire. My buddy laid his half on the stock of his gun while I cut a small stick and began roasting my half over the fire. The stick burnt in two, and the meat dropped in the fire. He laughed because I didn't get to eat any of the dove. Another dove flew over, and he picked up his gun to shoot it and dropped his half of the meat in the dirt. He didn't think it was funny when I laughed at him.

That fall Mom, my sisters, and I moved to Florida near some friends who had lived near us in Chicago. My friend Raymond and I would take his dad's .22 rifle out in the swamp and shoot squirrels, owls, and armadillos. I don't know if the season was open, but I know we didn't have a hunting license. Since there were poisonous snakes, I was looking for snakes on the ground more than I was looking up in the trees for squirrels.

We would go camping out in the orchards at night and have "grapefruit" fights. Once someone in the group got mad and started shooting at another's legs with an old Red Ryder, and everyone joined in. We finally called a truce and quit before anyone got hurt. Kids, don't ever do that.

I almost drowned that spring. My high school buddies and I were out on a cattle ranch at the edge of town after school one sunny afternoon. We would go there and rope and ride the yearling calves. We would drive them into the small corral, rope them, hog-tie 'em, get on, and turn them loose. If they wouldn't go back into the corral, we would chase them around the pasture. The rancher would have been mad as hell if he knew we were running all the fat off his calves.

One day the calves wouldn't go into the corral, and we were in the pasture standing next to a very large Brahma bull. My buddy said, "I bet you can't rope him." I did! He dragged all five of us hanging on the rope around the pasture and through all the dirt and fresh cow patties he could find. We ran him into the corral where we choked him down enough to get the rope off him.

We were all hot, sweaty, and dirty; so we decided to strip off jaybird naked and went swimming to wash off. The rest of my buddies could swim and wanted to swim back across the lake, back to our clothes. I started across and only got about one hundred feet from shore before going under three times. I swallowed a lot of water before my buddies got me pointed back toward shore. I was pretty humble as I walked back around the lake naked, all by myself, that day.

We moved to Springfield, Ohio, in the spring of 1955. My old Red Ryder wore out, so I could only shoot birds and pigeons with a borrowed pellet pistol. I bought a longbow and some target arrows and would shoot robins and squirrels in the city park. That summer, when I was visiting with my grandparents in Illinois, my friend Larry and I would go fishing and shooting frogs down by the creek. We were setting under the bridge and Grampa's rifle was empty, so I decided to load up and be ready when the frogs came back up for air.

I had the cartridge tube slide out and was putting cartridges in the rifle when I heard that horrible sound. It was a light rustling, sliding noise on the steel beam about a foot beside my left ear. Having played in barns and old buildings, I knew that sound could only be a snake slithering along the beam under the bridge.

I wasn't afraid of the nonpoisonous black snakes and blue racers but just coming from the poisonous snake country of Florida and Ohio, it caused me to gasp when I saw a two-tone brown snake sliding a foot in front of my eyes. I thought, Poisonous copperhead. I must admit I jumped back a foot or two to shoot from the hip, but the rifle wouldn't fire.

Raising the rifle up to my shoulder to shoot the snake, the rifle still wouldn't fire because it was empty. I tried to pump a new cartridge into the chamber, but the slide tube was out so the next cartridge wouldn't feed into the chamber. It was probably a good stroke of luck because that bullet would have ricocheted off the steel beam and caused quite a stir in the close quarters under the bridge for Larry and me.

The snake disappeared behind some dirt on the beam, and it gave me time to compose myself and load the rifle. The snake stuck its head out of a hole in the beam to drop into the creek when I shot, killing it. It was just a common water moccasin about three feet long.

In the summer of 1956, I got my first driver's license and stayed with my grandparents again and worked in my uncle Chris's garage washing cars and pumping gas. I bought my first car, a 1947 Plymouth four-door sedan for $125. Squirrel season was open. Dad took me hunting in the woods that I walked past every day going to school, about a mile from our old home place, and I shot a fox squirrel.

Another squirrel ran up a tree down in the woods, and we walked up to the tree, which had a big leaf nest in the fork of two limbs. I heard movement, and Dad told me to shoot into the nest. I killed two young raccoons. I didn't have a license to hunt, and I don't think the season was open for raccoon. Dad didn't like to hunt or fish and only took me hunting rabbits once before that time; I guess he didn't know much about game laws or cared to teach me right from wrong.

That fall, we moved to the small town of Greenfield, Ohio, and I cut grass to earn money to buy Sports Afield and Outdoor Life magazines and dreamed of hunting and owning guns to enjoy the sport. Old man Roy Ford, who lived in the downstairs apartment, took me hunting squirrel on his farm down in the hills below Bainbridge.

We had to drive past the small community of "Knock 'em Stiff" and "Do It and Run Holler." The names came from making moonshine in the bootlegging years. I shot a gray squirrel with his rifle, out of the top of a big beech tree, and was proud to bring home some food for the table even though the season was closed.

Roy's son Jim and I would roam the hills on weekends and would shoot anything that moved. Jim always wanted to smoke something out of a hole. Jim found a big hollow beech tree about three feet in diameter with a hole cut in the bottom of it. He stuck his head into the hole and said, "I think I see something." Jim always smoked and carried matches, and the next thing I knew, he had a fire going and smoke coming out of the top of the tree. I sat back with his .22 rifle and waited.

Nothing came out to shoot at, so we both took a whiz on the fire in the tree. We waited until the smoke stopped and then headed for home. The next weekend, we were back down in the hills again, and his grandmother asked if we had heard the news. She said, "A tree caught on fire and burned up a half acre of woods." Jim looked at me and said, "I'll be darn."

That fall, when I was 15, I bought my first rifle for $20, a used model 512 Remington .22 rimfire bolt-action rifle with a tubular magazine that held 12 long rifle cartridges. It was in excellent condition and had a smooth dark walnut stock and blued barrel. The rifle would shoot shorts, longs, or long rifles interchangeably from the magazine. Long rifle shells cost seventy-five cents and shorts only cost fifty cents for a box of fifty, so I mostly shot shorts. They were quiet and accurate out to fifty yards.

I could hit LGBs and dickey birds (little gray birds and song sparrows) with iron sights, offhand, at fifty yards just about every shot. I would buy a box of shorts and shoot about half of them every other evening after school down by Paint Creek. Except for shooting everything I saw, it did keep me out of more serious trouble and made me an expert rifle shot. I could throw a walnut in the air and shoot it with my rifle before it hit the ground.

I did some trick shooting one day with a bunch of my high school friends. We went out to the Old Maid's (Olie Due's) house to shoot starlings and pigeons. We were up in the hayloft of her barn when someone bet me I couldn't shoot a cigar out of my friend David's mouth. David was a senior and knew better then to light the cigar so he wouldn't catch the barn on fire; I figured he was smart enough to know what he was doing.

I was only a junior but knew better too. Kids, don't ever do this at home or anyplace else. David was at least twenty feet away, and I had a safe background of several bales of hay to shoot into. All the other boys stood behind me as I took aim at the middle of the cigar and squeezed the trigger.

David flinched as the tobacco bits hit him in the face. For a minute I thought I had hit him, but I didn't think that was possible because my rifle was sighted in to hit where I aimed at the cigar. It scared me bad enough not to ever try that again. Later I bought a four-power Weaver scope for $10 and could hit small targets out to one hundred yards. I bought a single-shot Harrison and Richardson .410 shotgun for $25 to shoot critters that flew and ran. It was a short light plain-looking shotgun; and the shot shells were little and easy to carry in the pants pocket.

It was a nice starter gun for a kid, but it didn't have the reach of a 12-gauge, and the quail were almost out of range by the time I got the gun up to my shoulder. Shotshells cost more than five boxes of .22 shorts, so I could get more enjoyment out of shooting the rifle. I shot groundhogs, doves, rabbits, squirrels, geese, and quail, mostly out of season.

In my spare time, I would read about being a government hunter or game warden in my magazines and dreamed about working in the great outdoors and using expensive guns. I got married in 1958, just six months out of high school, worked in building construction, and was laid off three weeks later; so I didn't have any extra money to buy any new guns. When my first daughter was born a year later in 1959, I sold the .410 shotgun and bought myself a model 721 Remington .270 bolt-action deer rifle and got laid off again the next week.

My mother-in-law had a fit because I spent money for a rifle when I had a wife and child to support. My father-in-law said that rifle would shoot a mile and that I was going to kill somebody. I told him I always knew where the bullet was going to land and not to worry. I worked odd jobs and paid my bills and we never wanted for food or clothes to wear, but that rifle put a strain on the marriage.

I just loved to hunt and be out in the woods and see wildlife. I guess that's why I still wanted to be a game warden. The local game warden, John Adams, lived a block from my house. I saw him at the county fair and talked to him about becoming a game warden. He told me to go to the Ohio Division of Wildlife Office and apply for a job, and they told me to get a college education than come back and they would hire me.

Working construction, going to college at night, and raising a family didn't work out, so I quit night school. Spring came, and I needed a rifle to shoot squirrels and groundhogs. The .270 cartridge was a little big for the quiet Ohio country-farming community. It was safe to shoot if there was a hill to stop the bullet, but the muzzle blast was too loud and noisy and would put all the whistle-pigs underground after the first shot.

I traded the .270 for a shotgun and then traded the shotgun for a model 722 Remington .244-caliber bolt-action rifle and put a ten power Weaver scope on it. The stock was a little short for my long arms and it looked like a club, but the rifle would sure blow things up. The 75-grain bullet would vaporize a crow or barn pigeon and take the head right off a groundhog. I would hunt west of town along the railroad tracks for groundhogs in the bean and alfalfa fields.

The railroad tracks crossed a bridge built over a big creek. The bridge was about three hundred feet long and about seventy-five feet above the water. The bridge had a small four-by-four-foot platform built on one side in the middle, where a fifty-five-gallon water barrel was set. I don't know what good it would be in the event the train caught on fire because a person couldn't get to it and walk on the bridge if the train was parked on it.

I had walked over the bridge many times when I hunted on the other side. On this particular Saturday afternoon, I parked my truck at the wide spot, at the road crossing, and listened for a train. I didn't hear any in the distance, so I walked out onto the bridge. I was standing, looking down in the creek at the fish, when I heard a noise behind me. I turned around, and a train was 150 feet away at the end of the bridge, coming my way.

The train didn't blow its whistle at the crossing as required or I would have been alerted earlier. I was just lucky I heard the noise when I did as I wasn't even halfway across the bridge, too far to run. I looked for the small platform, and it was still twenty feet away. I didn't want to jump seventy-five feet into the creek and break my neck or legs, so I turned and ran to the platform and just grabbed the railing when the train went rumbling past me.

I don't know if the engineer even saw me since he didn't blow the whistle or hit the brakes because I never heard the wheels screeching, trying to stop. It didn't scare me too much at the time as I stood there and waited for the train to cross and then went the rest of the way across the bridge and hunted groundhogs. I do think about it once in a while and thank the good Lord that I wasn't killed or crippled as I wouldn't be here today.

My poacher friend (I'll call him George) and I were hunting squirrels with his dogs one day during the closed season, and they ran a squirrel up a tree into a leaf nest in the top branches. I shot into it and killed two squirrels with one shot. George said I was just lucky. Many a time, I killed a limit of four squirrels with four bullets. Sometimes twice in one day!

Poachers say the poacher's hunting season is the week before the legal season, the week after, when it snowed for good tracking, at night, whenever the animal is giving you an easy shot by the road, or when the warden is off on a holiday.

George's dogs would also run deer when we were hunting rabbits. The deer season wasn't open, but he said it was always a good idea to have some rifled slugs for the shotgun in one's pocket, just in case a deer ran by. The dogs would chase the deer out of the area, and then we had to catch the dogs before we went home. George would blow through the barrel of his single-shot shotgun. It sounded like a trumpet, and the dogs would come running back to the car.

I worked with George, and sometimes he would stretch the truth a little. He said he went gigging one night, which was legal, for quillback, a rough fish. He said he gigged 64 fish, about 10 pounds each, then put them all, 640 pounds, in a coffee sack, which would only hold one hundred pounds!

Not to be outdone, I asked him if he heard about the hunter who killed a big buck in Adams County. I said, "When the hunter skinned the buck, he found it had been shot before. The hunter found seven .30-30 bullets, four 12-gauge shotgun slugs, a quart of buckshot, and ten pounds of arrowheads in it." George said, "Ah, damn you," and stomped off.

We would "noodle" catfish, which was also illegal, in August, when they were building their nests under the rocks. A person would put his hand in the hole to grab the fish and hope there wasn't a snake, muskrat, or turtle in the hole. If the hole was slimy, there wasn't any fish in it. If a catfish was building her nest, the bottom would feel like sand as she would keep it clean by fanning her fins for her eggs to hatch.

If a turtle was in the hole, you could tell which way it was facing by the three notches on the back of its shell. It was also a good idea to keep all your fingers together so a turtle wouldn't bite one of them off. We would have the fish tied on a stringer to our ankle under the water as we walked in the creek back to the truck. We could reach down and untie it if the warden came by, and the evidence would swim away.

Sometimes I would go to the dump along Paint Creek and throw cans and bottles into the creek. I would shoot my .22 rifle from the hip and hit most of them on the first shot; the rest I would hit with the second shot every time. I had a safe backstop for the bullets and the river was too deep for people to wade and they wouldn't get cut on the broken glass; however, it is not a good idea to litter or break glass bottles in the river.

I always worked hard for my employers, but building and road construction always came to a standstill during the cold months of winter. Unemployment checks were not big enough to support a family with three kids for very long. Working twelve-hour days and standing in concrete in rubber boots in the summer when it was a hot ninety-six degrees wasn't my idea of fun either.

I also remember working on my uncle's farm, the summer of 1951, when I was eleven. I got fifty cents a day and all I could eat when I helped milk the cows, feed the chickens and pigs, mow the grass, and pull weeds in the garden. If I helped bale hay, I was paid $1 a day. Those one-hundred-pound wire-tied hay bales weighed a pound more than I did. I was allergic to grain dust; and when I had to shovel oats or wheat into the grain bins, my eyes would water so bad I could hardly see what I was doing.

Working a whole month, I earned $20, which I used to buy a bicycle so I could ride the two miles to school every day. My older sister had a bicycle, but I had to carry my younger sister on my bicycle so she didn't have to walk. Illinois was pretty flat, but a couple small hills between our house and school seemed like mountains when I was peddling up them with her riding behind me.

Not wanting to be a farmer or have to carry bricks up a ladder or be pouring concrete when I was forty, I decided to look for another job.

A CAREER CHANGE

I liked law enforcement, but I didn't want to break up bar fights, chase cars, or investigate fender benders. Game protectors' starting salary was $330 a month. That was better than unemployment. I wanted to be a game warden. I knew how to poach, so I figured I would be good at catching the crooks. I lived next door to the local game warden, and he couldn't catch me. So, in order to protect the wildlife, the Ohio Division of Wildlife (ODOW) decided to hire me.

Well, it didn't happen exactly that way. Ohio was hiring a bunch of new game protectors, as they were called back then. After my neighbor John Adams told me to go to Columbus and put in an application, maybe I convinced them enough that I knew a little about wildlife and had the desire to enforce the laws and protect wildlife to take the test. I couldn't believe they suspected me of shooting all those groundhogs from the road.

During the next three months, I went to the library and took out every book I could find on fish and wildlife. I could identify all the different species of ducks and knew how many eggs they laid and how long it took for them to hatch. I knew what species of fish were in Ohio and where to catch them. I took the written test and scored number 1, on top of all the other applicants, and later passed the oral.

I poached my last wildlife, a pheasant killed during the closed season on New Year's Day 1965, the week before I went to the game warden training school. My wife's brother and I were hunting rabbits when the pheasant flew up in front of us. He shot at it and missed it. I didn't start the day with the intent to violate any game laws, but he shot at it and I naturally brought my shotgun up and shot too. I hit it and killed it.

When we went into the house for lunch, my three-year-old son asked, "Did you shoot anything, Daddy?" I held up the pheasant and said I shot a "flying rabbit." My son got excited and ran back into the house and said, "Daddy shot a flying rabbit." I know by now you are thinking I just admitted to another violation; however, the statutes of limitations are long past.

The next night John Adams, the game warden, came over to tell me the game protector training school would start the next week. I was trying not to be nervous while we sat and talked in the front room and hoped my son didn't come running in and say, "Daddy shot a flying rabbit," as it was still in the refrigerator in the kitchen. He didn't, and I ate the pheasant the next Sunday for dinner.

The Ohio Division of Wildlife hired me as a game protector, along with eighteen other cadets, on January 11, 1965; and I made a commitment to change my ways and protect wildlife and catch poachers from that day forward. And I did. My poacher friend George had taught me a lot about the ways of the woods.

I went to see him one last time to tell him I was going to be a game warden and that if I ever caught him, I would take him to jail. He said he wouldn't go to jail; he would shoot me first. I told him to make the first shot count. I never saw him again, and the local game protector never arrested him; so maybe he changed his way of life too.

I would ride with John, my neighbor, to the training school in Chillicothe, where he was the training officer. We stayed in the Department of Natural Resources' headquarters office building five days during the week. We would be there for twelve weeks, and the division administration staff and other officers taught us department policy, fish and wildlife identification, wildlife law enforcement, and search and seizure and arrest authority.

We had to march in files of two's a couple blocks down the street three times a day to the local café where we ate our meals. The town had a paper mill, and the air really smelled bad, like rotten eggs. So sometimes the food didn't taste as good as it should. The cook overheard someone complain about the food and came out of the kitchen and said, "All right, who is the smart-ass who said their steak was tough?"

She was a very large ugly woman with hairy legs and armpits, and she was wearing a dirty T-shirt. She also had a cigarette hanging out the corner of her mouth. I think it was my good old buddy Bob Ford who, with a big grin on his face, pointed over to me. The cook came over to my booth and was about to give me a piece of her mind when I said," My steak is just right." She grunted and left in a huff.

About the eleventh week, the other trainees and I were getting cabin fever, and we would arm wrestle to see who was the strongest. Having worked hard manual labor for the past six years, I won. One night, someone from my room decided to sneak into the other room and put some shaving cream on another trainee. We put a waste-paper can in front of the door to alert us if John was coming.

We were running back and forth between rooms in the dark and having a jolly good time when we heard the door hit the metal can. My friend Bob and I were out of position to get back into our beds and kinda got caught red-handed, so to speak, in our underwear in the hall. Everybody had to get up at 1:00 am and write affidavits for search warrants.

The next day, some of us were wrestling and I twisted my ankle real bad. Now I was worried I was going to get kicked out of training school before I had a chance to work in the field. Well, I made it to the last day and was sent over to Mercer County on the Indiana border to fill a vacant station. Another trainee was sent over to stay in the motel with me and then he would work in Darke County after training. This was flat farm country and the water tasted bad and I didn't want to go there.

Mercer County was only eighteen miles wide and twenty-nine miles long, but it had the biggest fresh water lake, Grand Lake Saint Mary's, in Ohio. Our field training was not very exciting as it was still cold in early March and there was not too much going on in the farm country. We only worked one night looking for raccoon hunters, and the ice was not strong enough for the ice fishermen to feel safe.

There was a waterfowl refuge on the lake, and we would drive around looking at the ducks and geese that didn't go south for the winter. We had lunch at a small café next to the lake and played cards for an hour every day with our training officers. They were in uniform but didn't seem to care as only the locals who knew them came in to see us. They had a short-timer's attitude. I can't remember writing even one ticket.

I was a hillbilly and didn't like the flat country, but I figured I could always transfer to the hill country after I finished probation. On the day we took our civil service exam, the old game protector, who was in Mercer County, decided he didn't want to take the promotion to wildlife agent. I wouldn't have to go back there. One of the other trainees took a job with the postal service and his station was vacant, closer to my hometown. I could go there. Please throw me in that briar patch.

When I was little, my grampa would tell me the story about the fox and the rabbit. The fox caught the rabbit one day and was going to eat him. The fox went past a briar patch on the way to his den. The rabbit said, "Mr. Fox, you can eat me, do anything you want, but please don't throw me into that briar patch." The fox thought the sticky briar patch would be a nasty place for the rabbit, so he threw the rabbit into it. The rabbit got away and lived happily ever after! Reverse psychology.

The Division of Wildlife Administration Office was located in Columbus with five regional offices in other parts of the state. Each region had a regional supervisor in charge of the supervisors of law enforcement and fish and wildlife divisions. The law enforcement supervisor was called a regional agent and supervised the wildlife agents, senior game protectors, and game protectors.

A game protector or senior game protector was assigned to each of the eighty-eight counties in Ohio to enforce fish and game laws, assist with fish and wildlife programs, pick up road-killed deer and nuisance wildlife, and attend sport club meetings to promote public relations. A senior game protector supervised three or four game protectors. The four or five wildlife agents in each region would investigate violations that took a long time to solve or required travel to other parts of the state. They reported directly to the regional agent.

My first station was south of Columbus, in Lancaster, on the edge of the rolling hills in Fairfield County. I had to carry a sidearm, so I bought a snub-nosed Colt .38 special pistol with a holster for $55 from John as he was going to be working in the office in Columbus. I never shot a pistol very much, but I could shoot pretty well with it.

The department gave me a green 1962 Ford Falcon car with over 100,000 miles for a patrol car. It would only go fifty miles per hour on the highway. The state had a contract with the highway department for gas and oil, and we had to fill up at one of their garages generally located in the county seat of each county. The oil was in fifty-five-gallon barrels, and we had to pump it into a quart can with a pour spout and pour it into the car ourselves.

I lived in a house with a daylight basement, and my patrol car didn't have enough power to back up the hill out of my garage. We didn't have decals on the door, but a green car with an eight-foot antenna and black state license plates had "game warden" written all over it. A dispatch radio operator worked out of the region office during the day and on opening day of deer season. We didn't have any communication during the night except car to car during the rest of the year.

Game protectors were limited to 1,500 miles during the hunting seasons and 1,000 miles a month the rest of the year. We could make an arrest for a violation that occurred in our presence, and the violators were issued citations or booked into jail. Then the officer had to file an affidavit with an official charge in the court the next day. I never took typing in high school, but I soon learned how by the hunt-and-peck method.

There was a prosecutor in each county with whom we could discuss violations that didn't occur in our presence or to obtain a search warrant. The prosecutor never appeared in court and didn't help the officer with a trail. If the violator asked for a hearing, the officer and the violator would just stand before the judge. We would raise our right hands and be sworn in and the judge would ask what happened. The officer would testify first about the facts and evidence, and then the violator would give his version of the event.

I can remember my very first arrest, a young man about my age was hunting groundhogs without a license along the railroad tracks at the edge of town. I knew how to play cards but didn't know much about routine patrol. I would drive around Fairfield County getting familiar with the roads and looked for hunters in the field or parked cars next to a wood lot. I was lucky I saw the hunter's car parked on the road next to the railroad crossing. He didn't have any identification with him, so I took him to jail to post $25 bail. That was the standard bail for small game violations back in 1965.

We were not issued handcuffs nor had any prisoner-transport policy, and I was a little excited, to say the least. I unloaded his rifle and asked him if he had any knives on him and placed him in the front seat beside me. The young man turned out to be the son of the Coon Hunters Club president. The president never held a grudge and said his son should have known better.

Fishing season was open all year, and fishermen could use two poles with two hooks per line. So the most common violation was for fishing without a license. I did make a few arrests for fishing with four poles. It was starting to warm up in the spring, and I encountered a lot of violations. Running back and forth patrolling the lakes and streams and filing affidavits in the neighboring county court made me drive three thousand miles and run way over my allotted mileage.

The regional supervisor saw me leaving the office one day and asked how I was doing, and I said I was catching a lot of fishermen without licenses. He said, "I see you drove three thousand miles last month."

I replied, "Well, I have to drive to all the different courts filing the affidavits."

He liked me, so he said, "Well, try to hold your miles down a little."

I also had to work in Columbus, handling nuisance wildlife complaints when my supervisor was on his days off. A woman called the office about a squirrel that got into her house by coming down her fireplace chimney. She fainted as she was talking to me on the telephone, and the line went dead. She called back in a few minutes and gave me her address so I could go and remove the squirrel. It was hard to catch.

One man called the office and said he had raccoons in the attic of his garage. I told him I would bring him a live trap and he could trap them and we would take them out into the country and release them. He wanted me to fix the hole in his garage. I told him to get a carpenter and fix the hole; the division would only provide the live trap. He was very upset that I wouldn't fix the hole in his garage too.

There were a few deer in the southern part of Fairfield County, and they would get hit by cars and killed on the roads. If the car owner didn't want the deer, I would have to field dress it and throw it on the trunk of my car and take it to the old folks' home at the edge of town or to the boy's reform school. They would process the deer meat for food for the residents to eat.

Fairfield County was irregular in shape and about twenty-three miles wide at the widest part and twenty-five miles long. It had Buckeye Lake where a lot of fishermen from Columbus would come to fish. The lake was on the county line with another new game protector, and my regional agent figured we both needed boat-handling training. He came out one day, and we practiced approaching boats and pulling up to the dock. The fourteen-foot aluminum boat with a twenty-five horsepower Johnson outboard motor had three seats with the steering wheel and motor controls in the middle of the boat.

We didn't have life jackets, just two boat cushions to sit on. We didn't have portable radios back then, but I think we had one wooden oar in case the motor quit on us. He thought we could use a little more training and recommended we take the boat out another day and get a little more practice.

One day the next week, I didn't have anything pressing to do, so I drove to the lake to get some more boat-handling practice. It was a cloudy day, and my buddy couldn't make it. There weren't any fishermen on the lake and I didn't swim well, so I was more than a little apprehensive.

I ran the boat down to the far end of the lake, and the wind picked up to about a twenty-mile-an-hour gale. So I headed back to the dock. The waves on the lake were now about four-foot-high, so I quartered the boat into the waves and held on for dear life. I stayed close to shore, but I thought the wind would tip my boat over and I would drown. This time I was in full dress uniform, but I was about as humble as if I was walking around that lake naked like down in Florida.

The people living on Buckeye Lake called the park office and reported my little problem, but the ranger didn't have a boat big enough to come and drag me back to the park office. I finally made it back and decided to be more observing of the weather the next time I went out.

On one of the holiday weekends, another officer and I were patrolling the lake. As we came around the corner of a small island, we observed a boatful of fishermen with everyone fishing with a pole in hand as we approached to check their license. We were in full dress uniform and wore a badge on our hat, but they seemed surprised when we asked to check their fishing license. One man, a nonresident, didn't have a license.

It was common practice if the violator had identification and lived in the local area, to issue a citation and let them go home. Nonresidents very seldom returned to the state to appear in court, so they were taken to jail to post bail or to be incarcerated until the next court date.

The violator was informed he would be taken to town to post bail. He said, "I am the governor's aide for Alabama." Nobody told me some people were exempt from the law, and he wasn't. I replied it was our policy to take nonresidents to post bail. He said, "I am an honorary highway patrolman." I again replied that it was our policy to take nonresidents to town to give them the opportunity to post bail. He could then call the court and set up a trial date if he wanted to contest the citation.

He finally got into our boat and his wife said, "I am going with him." We now had four people with only two boat cushions in the boat that was riding low in the water. I let them sit on the cushions just in case the boat sank. When we reached shore, I suggested his wife drive their vehicle and follow me so they would have a way to get home. I would only be taking them to the town and would not bring them back to the lake.

They said their friends would pick them up, and she rode in the back seat of my car. They never spoke during the ride to town. The violator posted $25 bail, and we departed. I wrote a report of the event and sent it into my supervisor. A couple weeks later, my regional agent saw me in the office and said the violator sent in a complaint letter and said I was very rude, ran a stop sign, and was speeding. I gave him my version of the contact, and my supervisor said, "Well, you learned one thing in training school. You sent in a report right away, so we weren't caught off guard by the complaint." Bait dealers who sold minnows and crayfish had to have a license. I saw a sign in the alley a block from the court house saying, "Minnows for Sale." I checked my records and didn't find a bait store in that area. I drove my personal car and walked in wearing a T-shirt and jeans. The man had live minnows in a tank, and I asked how much for a dozen. He said twenty-five cents. I told him I would take a dozen, the last of the big spenders.

I didn't want to buy a lot of minnows and then find out he just got a new bait dealer's license that I didn't know about. After I paid for the minnows, I produced my badge and identification and asked to see his bait dealer's license. He said he didn't get a license because he didn't know how many minnows he would sell. I issued a citation with a bail amount of $75. He went to court, and the judge fined him $25 after he bought a bait dealer license. My first undercover case.

That summer, six months after getting hired, I was offered a promotion to wildlife agent. My regional supervisor transferred over to another region and wanted me to come, too, and work for him. I had just bought a house in Lancaster and would have to move back up to the Indiana border and live and work in Mercer County, the area with the bad-tasting water.

I drove to Columbus and talked to my friend and training officer John Adams. John said it was an honor to get promoted in such a short time but I didn't have a lot of experience and there would be other promotions. I told John I really didn't want to go to Mercer County; I would rather live in the hills of Southern Ohio. He said, "Well, turn it down and wait for another promotion later." I turned it down, and the position wasn't filled.

The game protectors, who looked good in a uniform, would have to work at the state fair and help the kids try to catch catfish from a stocked pond. They would let fifty kids fish for ten minutes with a cane pole with a bobber and worms for bait. The kids could keep the fish and take it home. The fish was put in a plastic bag, and the kids would run around the fair the rest of the day in the hot ninety-plus-degree heat. By evening, the fish was pretty smelly and not fit to eat. My friend Bob Ford and I looked good in our uniform and would have to go and assist.

I finally got a new patrol car, a black 1965 Plymouth four-door sedan. It also had an eight-foot antenna and black license plates. The poachers soon learned it was the game warden's new car. One evening, about midnight, I was coming home from working spot lighters and pulled up to a stop sign in the center of a small town. I had my window down, and there were two teenaged boys standing on the corner about to cross the street. I heard one of them say, "Run, it's the cops." The other one said, "Nay, it's just the game warden." No respect!

The department wouldn't buy air-conditioning for us. When I parked the black car along the creek, in the ninety-plus-degree heat, to check a fisherman in the summer, it was like an oven when I had to get back in to drive again. I would roll the windows down and drive fast to the next bridge to get cooled off then lock the car up again and check more fishermen.

There was a family of poachers living in the last house at the end of a wooded hollow. The road was so bad I couldn't drive up the hill in my car as the state wouldn't buy us mud and snow tires. I would drive in from the backside of the hill from a paved road and set above their house and listen for shots during the closed season then drive back down the hill.

One afternoon I sat on the hill for a couple hours and didn't hear any shots, so I drove down past the house real slow and looked things over. I called it preventive enforcement. I then drove down the road to the covered bridge over the creek. Ohio had about thirty-two covered bridges in the state, and twelve of them were in Fairfield County. The bridges were unique and real sturdy, but the kids would kick out a board about midspan so they could jump into the creek to swim in the summer.

I drove into the bridge and looked up and down the creek out of the hole. The sixteen-year-old son (I'll call him Toby) of the poacher family was setting traps during the closed season a quarter mile downstream. I parked my car and walked downstream and contacted him. We pulled his traps and headed for the car. He didn't have any identification on him. He lied to me about how old he was and said he was only fourteen.

I told him I would take him back to his house and find out the truth. I knocked on the door, and his mother came to the door. I explained why I was there while Toby went in to get his driver's license. His younger brother came running into the room and yelled, "Hey, Toby, guess what? The game warden went by."

Toby said, "Shut up, damn it. He's outside." His mother was standing two feet in front of me, looking me in the eye, and it was all I could do to keep from laughing in her face. I cited Toby into juvenile court to appear before the judge, and he received a fine, doing fifty hours of community service.

I was picking up a lot of nuisance wildlife and didn't have anything to carry the critters in. A wire cage would let the urine and fecal matter get all over the trunk of my car, so I found a large old mailbox that I could carry in the trunk of my car. It was more sanitary and I put a snap in the lid and could lock it to keep the critters from getting out. I made myself a catch pole out of a five-foot piece of electrical conduit and an eight-foot piece of plastic-coated wire clothesline. I drilled a hole in the middle of a four-inch piece of broom handle and attached the wire to it.

Pulling on the handle kept the noose tight around the neck of a raccoon or possum while I put it in my carrying cage. Maybe I should have patented it for catching wildlife and would be richer today. I picked up a lot of baby raccoons and a few baby skunks. My kids would feed them and want me to keep them as pets. I would take the critters to someone who had a permit to raise wildlife in captivity or turn them loose into the wild.

One day I picked up a possum in Columbus and put it in the mailbox in my trunk. I was checking fishermen on the way home, and I forgot about it. It was about ninety degrees outside; I don't know how hot it was in the trunk of my car. I could hear a strange noise coming from the box, and I opened it up and found ten baby possums trying to nurse on the mother possum. I put them out along the creek as she looked pretty dead, then I thought, Maybe she was just playing possum?

I had to dispatch injured wildlife that had been hit and crippled on the road by cars, and I didn't want to carry my personal rifle in the state car. So I looked for a cheap .22 to carry behind the seat. My buddy and I went to the Columbus police auction for unclaimed guns and found a Winchester model 69A bolt action .22-rimfire rifle with a five-shot detachable clip magazine.

The screw that held the barrel to the stock was loose, and the gun rattled when I picked it up. I bid $10 for it, and nobody else bid on it. I bumped Dick on the arm and said, "I was going to get that rifle for $10." The guy behind me heard me and bid $11. I bumped the bid up to $12.50, a real big spender, and got the rifle. It was a cheap rifle to bump around in the state car, and my kids shot it when they got bigger. After I refinished the stock in 1993, it looked like a new rifle.

The game protector's duties also included presenting a program in the schools for career day, speaking at Chamber of Commerce meetings, and attending the local sports club to explain new seasons and laws and to promote good working relations between landowners and sportsmen. There were three clubs that I attended once a month: the Beagle Club, the Coon Hunters Club, and the Baltimore Sportsmen Club.

After the business meeting, the club president would say, "I see the game warden is here," and would then ask if I had anything to tell the members. I would go up front and talk about the fishing and hunting prospects or some special event that would be of interest to the members. Most of the members were very nice and interested in the information about wildlife.

The clubs always had a refrigerator full of beer and served food after the meeting. One meeting, a member was drinking a little too much and was talking loud in the back room and had disrupted the president all night long. When the president asked me to come forward, I overheard the drunk say "that damn game warden."

I was never one to shy away from speaking up to defend myself. I said, "Hey, buddy, if you have something to say, come out here so we can all hear it. If not, shut up so the rest of the member can hear what I have to say." It got so quiet you could hear a pin drop. I gave my presentation and never had another problem with that man.

In the spring, the game protectors had to assist the hatchery personnel pull the trap hoop nets on the big lakes and collect walleye eggs. It was always cold and sometimes raining, and a lot of the officers didn't want to do it. I liked seeing all the big fish and enjoyed helping when asked. After collecting the eggs, I would have to drive over a hundred miles one way to take them to the hatchery. I was proud to increase the fish population so that maybe a kid would enjoy catching them in the future.

The license year started on April 1, and in March, we had to go to the Columbus headquarters office and package and wrap the new books of licenses to mail out to all the license dealers. One of the older game protectors didn't like doing it and would mess up the orders on purpose so he wouldn't be asked to come back. I guess being efficient has its drawbacks.

The wildlife division would trap and band waterfowl in the winter, and I would help net the birds for banding. I also had a wood duck nest-box program in Fairfield County, and in the winter, I would walk on the ice and clean, fix, and erect new boxes. I would cut holes in the ice and drive an eight-foot metal post into the ground and attach a new box to the pole with bolts. In May, I would check the boxes and count the eggs and band the female duck if I could catch it in the nest box.

In June, I would count the eggshells left in the box after the ducklings hatched and submit a report on production. In the summer, I would set a wire live trap on the lake and bait it with corn and band the ducks I caught. In January each year, we had a midwinter waterfowl survey and had to identify and count all the ducks and geese we saw on the open water. I enjoyed doing these activities and getting a break from arresting people.

There wasn't a hunting season for quail or dove in Ohio, but in the spring, I would have to run dove coo counts and pheasant crow counts on a twenty-mile mile assigned route in Fairfield County. I had to start at daylight and stop for three minutes then drive a half mile and stop again. I would count all the dove and pheasants I heard and submit a report to get an index on the population. I liked hearing the first birds sing as the sun was coming up. It reminded me of hunting at daylight. The division of wildlife started a pistol team, and I qualified with my little Colt snub-nosed revolver. It wasn't a very good firearm to shoot in competition, so I traded it for a model 27 Smith & Wesson .357 mag revolver with a six-inch barrel. It was an accurate pistol, and one day, from a bench rest, I put three bullets in a two and-a-half-inch group at one hundred yards. Nobody was there to see it, but I still have the target.

The .357 was too big and clumsy to carry on my belt, so I traded it along with five dollars for a model 15 Smith & Wesson .38 special K 38 with a six-inch barrel. It was an accurate pistol, and my scores improved. One day I shot a bumblebee out of the air and head shot a groundhog at sixty yards. It made me feel good, and I had a witness both times.

The K-38's wide hammer spur and rear sight were always scratching my arm when I carried it on my belt in the summertime, so I bought a model 10 Smith & Wesson 38 special with fixed sights on a four-inch heavy barrel for $70 to wear with my uniform. It shot well and was easier to carry. A few years later, the department furnished our sidearms and holsters. I was one of the firearms instructors who helped train the other officers qualify with their new service revolvers.

I could outshoot the other officers most of the time. No bragging, that's a fact. I always kept my pistol clean and in good working order, but I would have nightmares about someone shooting at me and their bullets hitting all around me. I would pull the trigger of my revolver, and it wouldn't fire. I would wake up sweating a lot of nights as I dodged the bullets from their guns.

The rabbit season was open, and I walked out into a field to check three hunters. One of the hunters started cursing me as soon as I got close to them. He kept holding his shotgun in front of him in a threatening manner. The hair on the back of my neck stood up, and I was on high alert. I had my revolver on but would only draw it and defend myself if he pointed the shotgun at me. I was aware of the direction each shotgun was pointed and walked over to his buddy to check his license first and to get out from in front of Mr. Attitude with the shotgun.

I was now about three feet from the shotgun and I said, "I'll check your license too," and put my hands on Mr. Attitude's shoulders and took one step to my left and got behind him. If he tried to turn and point the shotgun at me, I would hold on to him and try to keep from getting shot.

He was still complaining about me being there and made a reference to the game warden that got shot and killed in another county about ten years ago. I was now on red alert and asked if he had written permission from the landowner, and he said no. I said, "Well, you have a license and are legal, but if you don't change your attitude, I can write you a ticket for hunting without permission." He settled down, but I kept talking to them as I backed away toward my car. I still remember that day.

I was getting to know the roads in the county pretty good and could drive just about anywhere without getting lost. I was checking coon hunters one night in the fall, around midnight, and was getting tired; so I pulled off the road by an abandoned farm woodlot. I went to sleep; but after a half hour, I started to wake up, and I could tell I was sitting behind the steering wheel of my car. I thought I was still driving and was going to run off the road. It scared the heck out of me, and I jumped, wide-awake, and grabbed the steering wheel before I realized I was parked and the motor was shut off.

Driving to another woodlot, I found a truck bearing Kentucky license plates with a dog box in the bed of the truck. I was standing between the driver's door and the car, resting my arm on the roof of the car and listening and waiting for the owner to return. It was as dark as the inside of a cave. Suddenly, I heard something behind me. I couldn't see anything, but I thought I saw something small moving up behind me on the ground.

I thought it was a skunk and jumped up over the spotlight, between the door and windshield, and up onto the hood of the car. I still couldn't see what it was, so I stepped back down into my car, got my flashlight, and shined it on a coonhound that had walked up to within five feet of me. We both had a surprised look on our face. I didn't realize I could jump that high, that fast.

It was now Sunday morning and illegal to hunt. I could hear more dogs barking in the woods and could see a light shining up into the trees but didn't hear any shots. After another hour, a man and a couple more hounds came walking out of the woods. He had a light and a .22 rifle and his dogs had treed a raccoon, but he couldn't find it in the tree. He was a nonresident and a preacher, of all things, hunting without a license. I cited him for hunting without a nonresident license and for hunting on Sunday, and he followed me to jail where he posted $75 bail.

Another night, I was again checking coon hunters and heard some dogs barking in a woodlot about a half mile off the road. I walked quietly to the woods and was standing about forty feet behind two hunters shining a spotlight up into the tree. One of the dogs smelled me and walked to within ten feet of me and started growling. I shined my light on the hunters and said, "State game protector," and walked up to the men.

After checking their license, one man said, "That dog was going to chew you up."

I said, "No, he wouldn't."

The man said, "Yes he would. He is mean."

I said, "No, he wouldn't. If he got past these binoculars"— which I showed him in my hand—"I would shoot him."

The man said, "You wouldn't shoot my dog."

I never told him if I would shoot or not. I just said, "He won't chew on me."

There were a lot of coon hunters in Ohio, and I worked a lot of nights checking them. I saw a truck parked by some woods at about 2:00 am, and I could hear dogs barking and see a light shining up into a tree. I waited by the truck, and pretty soon a man with a .22 rifle and two dogs came out of the woods. He didn't have a hunting license, and I issued him a citation for hunting without a license with a bail amount of $25.

He said, "Man, I didn't think you would be working this time of night." He later forfeited $25 bail. When I was little, my grampa told me the story of the fox and the little red hen. The fox was always trying to catch the red hen when she went to the market. The red hen would get up real early and be back home before the fox got up. The next day, the fox got up real early, and the red hen went real late after the fox went home.

A game protector has to be self-motivated as they are basically their own boss. Unless they had court, training, or a meeting to go to or working with another officer, their main decision of the day was where to patrol. Fishermen were easy to find as the season was open all year. Hunters were harder to find, depending on the species being hunted.

I figured if I wanted to catch a poacher, I had to get up earlier than they did and stay out longer. That system seemed to be working. I was getting to be known by the coon hunters, and when I shined my light on them, they would ask, "Is that you, Holste?" It made me smile when I replied, "Yeah."

There were also fox hunters in Ohio that would park in the hills at night, build a fire, and let their hounds loose to run fox all night. I would get complaints about their hounds running deer, but it was pretty hard catching them in the act. It was hard to tell the foxhounds from the coonhounds. The hounds would run coon, fox, or deer if the track was hot.

One spring night in May, I saw a car parked by a small lake before the frog season was open. I pulled in behind it with my headlights turned off and parked. I got out and walked up to the lake in the dark to see if someone was fishing or frog gigging. Pretty soon I saw a cigarette glow in the dark when a man took a puff on it. A flashlight came on, and I could see two men that were standing working on a frog gig.

A bullfrog would bellow, and the man would shine his light on it and then back on to the frog gig he was working on. After they fixed the gig, they walked toward me and gigged the bullfrog. They speared the frog, and I shined my flashlight on them and said, "Game protector. You're under arrest." They had a sack full of frogs, and I issued them both citations for taking frogs during the closed season. They came to court and were each fined $50. The headlines in the newspaper read, "Froggy Goes a Court-en."

I was checking fishermen on Buckeye Lake and observed three men fishing for catfish back in a slough. They were fishing with worms on the bottom without a bobber. Two of them each caught a catfish, and the third was sitting and holding his pole, trying to catch a fish that was pulling on his line. When he saw me approach, he cut his line as he didn't have a license. When I issued him a citation, he said he didn't have a hook on the line. I asked him, "Then why did you cut the line?" He wouldn't answer.

The three of them came into court and lied to the judge and claimed the violator only had a sinker on the line and was practicing casting since he didn't have a license. The judge asked him, "Then why did you cut the line when the officer came up?" He said it got caught on a rock, so he cut it to get it loose. There were three of them lying and only one me.

The judge just rolled his eyes and said, "Well, I'll find you not guilty. You get yourself a license before you go practicing again." I was a little upset at them for getting away with lying in court under oath and that the judge knew it too. I couldn't do anything about it.

That was the first case that I lost.

It was illegal in Ohio to possess wildlife unless it was taken lawfully during an open season. One day during the summer, I walked past a car parked in town and observed a raccoon tail tied to the car radio antenna. A lot of hunters put a fox tail on their antenna, which is legal since the season was open all the time. Some raccoon hunters would also put a coon tail on their antenna during the winter from a legal kill.

This raccoon tail smelled when I walked by as if it was from a fresh kill. The raccoon season had been closed for three months, so I waited a short distance away up the street until the owner came back. When the owner came back to put more money in the meter, I approached him and asked about the raccoon tail, and he started getting real nervous.

The flesh on the tail was fairly fresh and smelled bad. He was a local coon hunter. I told him that the tail appeared to be from a recent kill and he said, "I found it." This was also illegal, so I issued him a citation for possession of wildlife during the closed season. He later forfeited $50 bail.

The game protector in the county north of me moved to another region, and a new officer was hired to take his place. I met the new game protector in the Columbus office when he was picking up his new equipment. We both headed home later, and he was following me. He asked over the car radio, "How do you get out of here?" I was stopped at a red light and I replied, "Just follow me." I turned right, and he followed.

About that time, I realized I was going down a one-way street the wrong way! I said, "Pull over." There was a police officer standing in the middle of the block looking the other way, and he didn't see us. We made a U-turn and headed back to the stoplight without causing an accident or getting arrested. It appeared I still didn't know the city that well either.

In 1967 ODOW wanted to win the NRA Hunter Safety Award by instructing more students in firearm safety than any other state. All the game protectors were assigned to train a quota of 150 students. I advertised the class dates and locations on the radio, put it in the newspaper, and announced them at all the sports clubs' meetings. I was only able to train fifty students in five classes. I had to assist my supervisor with his class of five hundred students in Columbus. He counted all the students for himself and wouldn't give me any, so I didn't reach my 150 quota.

Back then we weren't given an evaluation. If we worked hard, made lots of arrest, and didn't have too many complaints about our work ethics, the supervisor stayed off our backs. The regional supervisor called me in to the office one morning and asked me why I only trained fifty students. I told him I made a good-faith effort and only fifty students came and attended the five classes I held in Fairfield County.

When I worked construction, I would try and do my best to cut a straight line or finish concrete perfectly every time. I always tried to do my best at any job I had to do. I was always on time to meetings and always had on a clean uniform and proud to represent myself and ODOW to the public. He wasn't satisfied with my explanation and demanded that I train more students. I told him I assisted my supervisor with five hundred students and didn't receive any credit for helping him with them.

He still wasn't satisfied. I said, "Sir, I made a good-faith effort. I attend more club meetings, do more work with the fish and wildlife divisions, and make more arrests than my supervisor or any other officer in my unit. If he can't or won't give me credit for some of the five hundred students I helped train, then he can just chew my a—." I was man enough to take it. I thought the regional supervisor was going to fall out of his chair. He said "You can't talk to me that way," and then said, "Wait here," and left. He came back about twenty minutes later and said "The chief wants to see you."

Each division had a chief and assistant chief who gave direction to the regional supervisor. His office was on the other end of the building in Columbus, so I didn't have far to go. I went into his office and explained the whole thing over again to him. He wasn't satisfied either. I said, "Sir, I have a good working relations with the people in Fairfield County. I am a good, honest person and represent the division and my position well with the public.

"I work hard with the other divisions, make more arrests then most of the other game protectors, and made a good-faith effort to get the 150 students by holding five training classes. The students just didn't come to my classes this year. I can't force them to come and take the class."

If he couldn't give me credit for some of the five hundred students I helped train, he could chew my a-- too. I was man enough to take it. He wasn't happy with my answer either and said, "We'll see what we are going to do about this," and I left.

The pistol team was going to the national combat matches in Bloomington, Indiana, the next week. Then we would assist as range officers at the Camp Perry matches for two days the next weekend. My supervisor sent me a letter and advised me that I was not to attend the Camp Perry matches as punishment for not getting my 150 students quota. I didn't care as we just stood around, but I was so mad about the whole process that I won the 1967 National Combat Sharpshooter Pistol Championship.

The assistant chief was also on the pistol team and asked me, "What made you shoot so good?" We were good friends, and I told him I just wanted to show the SOBs in the office that I was one of the best game protectors in Ohio. He probably helped talk the rest of the staff into letting me attend the national matches in Indiana since my entrance fees were already paid.

Things cooled off after a while, and I was back to making a lot of arrests. An old widow living ten miles south of town would always call and report poachers. She owned forty acres of timber, and the hunters would sneak in from a piece of vacant property next to hers and hunt squirrel and deer. Her bedroom was in the front of the house, and she could also see cars going by and spotlighters when they shined her fields at night. She would call, and by the time I got there, the poachers would be gone. She was on a party telephone line, and the neighbors would listen in and know when she called.

Trophies from police combat shooting

The legal shooting hours were from 9:00 am to 5:00 pm. During the deer season, I was checking hunters around the corner from her house one evening. I was waiting for a deer hunter to come out of the woods back to his car. I had coveralls on over my uniform, and this was before I carried my black broomstick; so I put my shotgun in the cradle of my arm and stood about fifty yards in the timber. I could see the road and also a little deeper into the timber from my position.

The hunter came out a little before quitting time and thought I was another hunter. He said, "Boy, I saw a big buck about 8:30 this morning."

Since the legal shooting time was 9:00 am, I asked him, "Did you get a shot at it?"

He said, "I would have, but that game warden stays just over the hill."

I think I might have had a grin on my face as I said, "Well, I am that game warden," and showed him my badge on my uniform. I said, "I would like to check your license." He was legal. I liked working undercover.

One evening a man called my house and asked if I was the game warden. I said yes. He said he had killed a hen pheasant during the hunting season last fall and wanted to turn himself in.

I said, "This is a joke, right?"

He said, "No, I can't sleep at night and I wanted to turn myself in and get it off my conscience." I could tell he was serious; so I asked him where he lived, and he gave me his address.

I made arrangements to stop by his house the next day. I wasn't very experienced at questioning, interviewing, or interrogating a suspect as most of my arrests had been from violations that occurred in my presence. I had watched Dragnet and Sergeant Friday on TV and figured this man wanted to turn himself in, so this should be fairly easy. I met him at his house and introduced myself and asked him to come out to my car and I would get some information from him.

I asked him if he still had the hen pheasant, and he said no. He didn't want to be caught with it, so he had buried it in the cornfield that same day. I told him this was an unusual case and I didn't witness the violation and didn't have any evidence. I asked him if he was trying to set me up for a false arrest. He said no. He had found religion and was having trouble sleeping at night. This was the only thing that he could think of that might be causing him to lose sleep.

I told him I would take the information to the prosecutor since I didn't witness the violation and see if he wanted to charge him with shooting a hen pheasant during the closed season. He could then appear before the judge and explain his case or post a $50 bail and forfeit the money and the case would be closed. He said he didn't want to come into court; he just wanted to pay a fine and get it over with.

I told him if he forfeited the $50 and didn't violate any more game laws, the case would be closed as far as I was concerned. He still might not be able to sleep at night. It would be up to the good Lord to forgive him. I didn't have that power. He thanked me, shook my hand, and I left. I contacted the prosecutor the next day and explained the circumstances to him, and he laughed and said, "If he wants to forfeit $50, I'll file the case."

The man paid the fine, and I never saw him again. After I submitted the case report, my regional agent saw me in the office and called me Preacher Bud. It seemed I had a way to get violators to tell me what happened. Another man called me and reported a car stopped in front of his house and a man stuck a rifle out the passenger window and shot a fox squirrel out of the tree in his front yard.

He had the car license plate number. I ran the registration and contacted the suspect at his house. He didn't want to come out to my car, so I interviewed him in his house. He was sitting in a chair across from me and wouldn't tell me who was with him or who shot out of the passenger-side window.

When questioned, he continued to lie to me. He was too comfortable sitting in his home; I should have had him come out to my car to question him. He reminded me of my poacher friend George. I told him that the property owner saw him and to get out his driver's license.

He gave me his license, and I got out my ticket book. His eyes got real big. I started writing out the citation and asked him if that was the only squirrel he shot, and he said yes. His wife was driving the car and he was riding in the passenger seat when the squirrel ran up the tree. It was the only one they saw that day, so he shot it. He forfeited $50 bail.

The first thing I look at when I check a license is the length of residence in the state then the DOB and height and weight. In Ohio, the hunters have to wear and display their hunting license in the middle of the back on the outer garment. I was checking two rabbit hunters, both around forty years old. The one subject's license said he had lived in Ohio for eighty-seven years.

I asked him, "How old are you?"

He replied, "What does it say?"

I said, "I am asking you."

He said he didn't have a license and saw his dad's coat with his hunting license lying by the door, so he took it and went hunting. I issued him a citation for hunting without a valid license. He forfeited $50 later in court. I saw my regional agent in the office the next day, and I told him I had arrested an old man using his dad's license. He asked, "How old was he?"

I said, "Forty-something."

He said, "I'm forty. That ain't old."

I replied, "Well, I'm twenty-six. He was older than me."

It had snowed a couple inches one night in December, and the next day I was driving up a steep hill during the deer season to check hunters. I was halfway up the hill when the wheels on my car started spinning and I couldn't go any farther. I was in the middle of the road, and the car just sat there with the wheels spinning and was starting to slide backward down the hill on the snow. I put the car in park, and it still slid backward.

I stepped out and pushed on the left front fender, and the car slid to the right. I thought it was going into the ditch, but it went past the ditch and was now headed back down the road. I got in, put it in gear, and drove on down the road. I complained to my supervisor, and other officers did too; so after three years, the state started buying mud and snow tires for our cars.

I had checked a group of deer hunters in the south end of the county above the Old Maids house before lunch, so I drove over to another area to work that afternoon. Right before quitting time, I checked a known deer poacher who just happened to be legal this time. He was hunting with the group I had checked in the morning. That evening, about 9:00 pm, I got a call from a man who wouldn't identify himself. He said there was a poached doe lying up in the hills above the Old Maids house and insisted that I go and get it.

I figured it was one of the poacher's friends giving me the runaround and wanted me to go to the south end of the county. I called the game protector in the next county and told him about contacting the poacher today and the phone call. I asked him if he would meet me in the north end of the county and work a couple hours to see if the poachers were up there poaching. He met me, and we worked until midnight. I just got home when the telephone rang again, and it was a voice I recognized. The man asked me if I got that doe and I said no.

The man insisted that I go up into the woods and get it. I replied, "There isn't any dead doe up in the woods. You are just giving me the runaround."

I said, "If you hold on a minute, I'll tell you who you are," and then I said, "You're Joe."

The man on the phone said, "You old SOB, how did you know that was me?"

I said, "I recognized your voice."

He said, "After I checked their group twice in one day, they figured I was following them."

I told him I had checked them in the morning and they were all legal, so I went to another area to work in the afternoon. Joe said, "Well, they didn't see any deer in the first place they hunted that morning, so they moved to another area that afternoon."

I told him, "Well, Fairfield County is a small area and I wanted to check other hunters, so I moved too."

Joe said, "You know, you're all right and a pretty good guy after all." He said he was sorry he gave me the runaround.

My paycheck wasn't going as far as I wanted it to, so I asked my supervisor if I could take a part-time job to earn some extra spending money. They said they didn't care as long as I took care of all my poaching complaints. I worked in a grocery store four blocks from my house stocking soap products from 11:00 pm to 4:00 am five nights a week. I would sleep a few hours and then go to work for the state during the day. It was springtime, so I didn't get any deer poaching or spotlighting calls.

I was burning the candle at both ends, so to speak, but could still check lots of fishermen and made a lot of arrests for fishing without a license and didn't have any complaints. So I was surprised when I was called into the office. The regional supervisor told me to go to the front office and see my friend the training officer. I was surprised when he asked, "How would you like a promotion?"

I was able to hunt small game, squirrel, rabbit, grouse, and turkey on my days off. I also hunted white-tailed deer with my bow in Michigan, Pennsylvania, Ohio, and West Virginia. I didn't put any meat in the freezer as I always wanted a bigger trophy and passed up numerous shots at does.

PROMOTION TO WILDLIFE AGENT

Well, I wanted a promotion, but it was the same position that I was offered three years ago in Mercer County. I said I was interested but would like to talk it over with my wife and family. I would work out of the region 5 office in Xenia. I asked if I could fill one of the vacant positions in region 4, and they said no. I didn't realize that politics were so strong in the division of wildlife. It seemed whatever this regional supervisor wanted, he got. He wanted me three years ago.

I didn't have to take an exam or compete against other officers for the position, so I guess I should be thankful and honored that someone thought I deserved the opportunity to move forward. I was thankful to be able to work at a job that I enjoyed and to be succeeding without a college education. It made me humble; it was almost more than I could believe. I always worked hard and tried to set a good example to others and figured the money would come with experience.

It would be a nice pay raise for me, so I decided to take the promotion. I was officially promoted to a wildlife agent's position on July 29, 1968, with a starting salary of $3.45 per hour. I drove over to Xenia to meet the regional supervisor and regional agent, my direct line supervisor. We worked out a deal. I would rent an apartment and work five days in a row and could drive back home on my days off in the state car until I could sell my house. I was supposed to work some weekends, but since I didn't receive routine calls anymore, I could work my investigation when it fit into my schedule.

I grew up in a small town and liked the slower pace of life, and then I had to work in and around Columbus. The biggest city in the state. I rented a furnished apartment in the small town of Pleasant Hill, about twenty miles north of Dayton. At least I would work in smaller cities and

investigate violations in Auglaize, Darke, Mercer, Miami, and Preble
Counties. There were two other wildlife agents who worked other counties
in the region.

The wildlife division filled other vacant positions, so they sent all
the wildlife agents for training at the Ohio Bureau of Criminal
Investigations. That was a real positive start for professionalism for our
law enforcement division. The training included interviewing suspects and
report writing. A very important point was to write it down right away
because tomorrow it would be hard to remember what had been said
yesterday.

Next month it would be hard to remember all the facts, and next
year it would be as if it didn't happen. The ODOW only furnished the
game protectors with a flashlight, binoculars, a uniform, a car, a boat, and a
file cabinet for his house to keep department forms and records. They still
didn't provide any tire chains.

The wildlife agents didn't have a boat, but they did have all the
other equipment plus a Polaroid camera, a box of a dozen quart glass jars,
and a pollution kit to sample the dissolved oxygen levels in the water when
collecting samples working on pollution and fish kills. We had a little
bigger travel-expense budget and mileage allotment as we had to drive
more to contact violators. We could also work out of uniform and with the
game protectors on routine boat patrols and special night patrols.

My friend Bob Ford quit in 1967 and moved out west to the state
of Washington to work for the game department. We stayed in touch with
each other, and he wanted me to apply for a job in Washington. I told him I
had just been promoted and still owned a house in Lancaster so I would
think about it in the future.

If I wasn't working on an investigation or interviewing a suspect, I
would go to the office and type reports.

A man who had a permit to keep deer in captivity called the office one day and said someone cut his fence and took one of his deer. About the same time, a police officer in the small town called and said he stopped a van for a traffic violation and it had a dead deer in it. Another wildlife agent and I were in the office, so we drove twenty-five miles to the police department office and interviewed the suspects.

The suspect that I was interviewing lied to me and said they found the deer dead on the road. He said he was in a motorcycle accident a couple years ago and had both legs broken. One leg broke in thirteen places and the other in fourteen places. He showed me the scars on his legs and said he couldn't walk for a year. He said he found religion after he was able to walk and wouldn't have killed the deer. I told him the deer was private property but still a game animal, the season was closed, and he couldn't kill it without permission from the owner.

I told him he better dig a little deeper into his religion and tell me the truth. He finally admitted that he and his buddy were drinking and they cut the fence and caught the deer and killed it with a ball-peen hammer. The other suspect was lying to my buddy until I explained all the facts about killing the deer. He finally admitted helping kill the deer. Both were charged with possessing a deer during the closed season. They didn't appear in court to contest the case and both forfeited $100 bail.

It seemed like every country road had a wide spot on a curve or along a creek and people would dump their garbage there. I would take a picture of it then dig through the garbage and dirty diapers to try to find a name and address of a suspect. I would then attempt to locate the suspect and obtain a confession and arrest them for litter. It seemed like they would always move after dumping the garbage and be hard to locate.

At one location, the only thing I found that would lead to a suspect was a year-old dog tag. I contacted the county clerk's office and found who bought the license. The suspect admitted dumping the trash, and I issued him a citation and contacted the prosecutor and filed a charge in court for littering. The suspect later forfeited $50 bail.

The game protectors in the north part of the region didn't turn in many complaints for me to work on, so I always had to drive down to the other end of our region, in Southern Ohio, to work. Catching closed squirrel hunters was a big thing back in Ohio. They would walk into the woods by going out the back door of their house, shoot the squirrels, and would return home before the game warden arrived. They were very hard to catch.

Someone called the office and reported hearing shots during the closed season. My supervisor drove his car and dropped me off by a car parked beside the woods. My poacher buddy George would always hide his rifle and the squirrels before coming out to the road back to his car. So I walked into the woods and my supervisor drove down the road and waited until I came back out onto the road.

I was able to make contact with the squirrel poacher before he hid his rifle and squirrels and took him out to the road and his vehicle. My supervisor drove up, and we took him to jail where the poacher posted $50 bail. Everybody in the office thought it was a big deal catching the closed season squirrel poacher. I felt like I had just caught my old buddy George.

Another call came into the office about a couple of hound hunters living in Dayton that were killing young raccoon to train their young dogs during the closed season. We didn't know where they hunted, so we were going to try and follow them. My supervisor was driving, and I rode shotgun in the passenger seat to read the road map and help navigate.

I could also jump out when they entered the woods. We were sitting a block from the suspect's house just before dark with a jacket over our uniforms. Some kids came up and asked, "Are you guy's cops?"

I said, "No, go play someplace else."

The suspects loaded their dogs into their truck and pulled out just before dark. We started out following them without using our headlight. If a car met us on the road, we would pull over and stop. We followed the suspects for about twenty miles without having a wreck or losing them. They pulled into a lane that ran off the highway toward a block of timber a quarter mile back in a field. They stopped by the woods and shut their truck lights off. I thought they would turn their dog loose and hunt.

I jumped out and ran across an open plowed field, and my supervisor parked in an old driveway. I was about halfway to the woods when the suspects turned their lights back on and drove in a circle, trying to see if anybody was following them. They were pretty smart. I was standing in the open field, so I fell on my back so they couldn't see me and, in doing so, ripped the rear end out of my pants. The suspects started to drive back toward the highway, so I got up and ran back to our car. We were able to catch up to them before they got out of sight.

We followed them for another half hour, and my supervisor asked me, "Where are we?"

I said, "I don't recognize anything." Then we saw an Indiana road sign and I said, "We are about six miles into Indiana." By a stroke of luck, the suspects turned around and drove back into Ohio. They stopped by another woods, and we drove a mile past them and turned around.

I got out by their truck as my supervisor drove real slow, then he parked down the road and waited. I got out just in time to hear the dogs bark treed and saw a light shine up a tree in the middle of the woods and then heard a .22 rifle shot. I heard an object hit the ground and the dogs get real excited fighting something. I was standing by the fence between the truck and the woods. The suspects hollered at the dogs and turned out their light, and I could hear them walking back to the truck.

A hound walked up and stood beside me. I was glad he didn't bark and give my presence away. When the suspects were about ten feet from me, I shined my flashlight on them and said, "State wildlife agent." They were surprised to see me, and the second man threw the rifle he was carrying down and came up to the fence. The man in front said, "We were just training our dogs. We didn't see anything."

I crawled over the fence and picked up the rifle. I told them, "I heard you shoot. Let's go back there and pick up the raccoon." The man wanted to put the dogs up first and insisted they hadn't shot anything. I told him that I probably couldn't find that raccoon in the dark but the dogs could and that we were going back to the tree with the dogs. They didn't want to go, but we went back close to where I saw the light. The dogs went over to a log, and there lay a dead raccoon.

Picking up the dead raccoon, I said, "You're both under arrest." My supervisor saw me turn on my flashlight and headed our way and was parked by the truck when we walked back to the road. I advised the suspects that they were going to jail to post bail. We could do it two ways. We could take them in our car and have their truck towed or I would hold their driver's license and they could follow us to jail in their truck. They followed us and posted $50 each and later forfeited bail.

The game protectors down by the Ohio River east of Cincinnati were having an emphasis patrol the week before the squirrel season opened, and I went down to help them. I had been working long days and was lying on the hood of my car near a woods where I heard a lot of shooting the year before. My head had been resting on a boat cushion since daylight, and I was starting to get sleepy.

About 10:00 am, the sun was getting warm and my eyelids were pretty heavy, maybe even closed, when I heard a .22 rifle shot in the distance. I sat up and looked in the direction of the shot, at a woodlot about a half mile away. I put on my camo coat over my uniform; and since I was living away from my home and didn't have access to my rifle or shotgun, I had started carrying a black broomstick. I entered the woods where I heard the shot come from and looked around. I didn't see anyone and after crawling through a lot of blackberry briers, I was thinking to myself that this wasn't a very good place to be hunting squirrel.

With the broomstick cradled in my arm, I looked like a hunter too, and a man said, "Howdy," and scared the hell out of me. He was sitting under a small tree about thirty feet away with a .22 rifle cradled in his arm. I ask him if he got the squirrel and he said no.

I asked him if it was a gray or fox squirrel and he said, "Gray squirrel." He said it was in the small hickory nut tree about thirty feet to my right. I walked over to him and laid my black broomstick down in front of him, and his eyes got as big as marshmallows.

He would look at the stick and then at me and then back at the broomstick. I showed him my badge and said, "You're under arrest." He said, "Damn it, I overslept this morning and got a late start and almost didn't come." I arrested him for hunting squirrel during the closed season and hunting on Sunday and took him to jail to post $100 bail, which he later forfeited. The other wardens asked me how I caught him, and I told them I just walked into the woods and he gave himself up!

A couple days before squirrel season opened another wildlife agent and I were working together in the same general area. We were parked next to an old barn on an abandoned farm. We were sitting on the hood of his car, and my buddy was eating an apple. I heard a .22 rifle shot about a mile north of us. He said he didn't hear it because he was chewing on the apple. The flatter part of Ohio is divided into square mile sections with a road all around it.

I said, "Well, let's drive to the next road and see if there is a woods close by." On the next road, there was an old run-down house sitting next to a block of timber. I jumped out of the car as my buddy slowed down, and then he drove off. He would drive back up the road and try to get between the woods and the house to intercept the poachers, in the event I missed them.

I had my camo coat over my uniform and I walked about fifty yards into the woods. It was the end of August and real hot. I was starting to sweat with the extra clothes on. I couldn't see anyone, so I sat under a maple tree. The mosquitoes were real bad, so I pulled off a big leaf and was twitching it back and forth in front of my face to keep from getting bitten up by the little pests.

I heard a shotgun blast about fifty yards in front of me, and a man with a shotgun stood up and walked around a big beech tree. Another man stood up with a .22 rifle and pointed it up into the tree and shot. A fox squirrel fell out of the tree, and the man with the rifle went over to it and picked it up. They were both admiring it and didn't hear me walk up until I was about twenty-five feet away from them. The man pitched the dead squirrel over his shoulder when he saw me.

Opening my coat and showing them my badge, I said, "State wildlife agent. You're both under arrest." They were hunting out of the house and didn't have any identification on them, so we walked back to the house. My buddy who was hiding in the tall weeds behind the outhouse stood up when we approached. The man with the shotgun lived in the house and was issued a citation for hunting squirrel during the closed season, with a bail of $50, and then released. The man with the rifle was a nonresident from Kentucky and was taken to jail to post $100 bail.

After we were back in the car leaving the jail, my buddy said when he heard the shot, one of the kids playing in the yard had said, "Daddy got another squirrel." I said maybe we should have searched the house and found more squirrels. The man from Kentucky later appeared in court and said he wasn't hunting. After I explained the facts and produced the squirrel, the judge found him guilty and fined him $75. I was getting pretty good at catching these squirrel poachers.

The waterfowl season opened on Saint Mary's Lake in Mercer County, and a game protector and I were working undercover to see if the hunters were shooting over their limits. The parks department issued permits for hunters to build blinds on the lake before the season opened. The blinds were built about a quarter mile from the waterfowl refuge on the south shore of the lake. The hunters would put out their decoys and shoot at the ducks and geese as they flew back and forth to the refuge and the open water.

We patrolled the back sloughs of the lake at daylight by boat, and it sounded like a war, with over fifty shots in less than a half hour. We were checking hunters on foot and had checked several hunters when a man came up to us and said, "You want to watch it. There is a game warden around here."

I replied, "Well, I'm that game warden, so I better check your license." He was surprised but was legal. We then found an empty blind where we could sit and look like hunters and watch the other blinds. We used our binoculars to see if anybody was shooting too many ducks or geese. We would then go over and check the hunters in the other blinds.

We both had our 20-gauge double shotguns along, so when we stood up, the other hunters would not be suspicious of us while we watched them. We both had hunting licenses and duck stamps. The 20-gauge was a little on the small size for pass shooting at the big geese, but we could shoot at a duck if it came close enough. It was a warm bright sunny day, which makes for poor waterfowl hunting. A lone Canadian goose flew by, and we both stood up. My buddy shot at it and missed. I shot at it, and it rocked back and forth but didn't go down.

My buddy fired his second barrel at it and missed again. I fired my second barrel at it but couldn't tell if I hit it. The goose flew about a hundred yards and dropped dead into the lake, so we took the boat and retrieved it. There wasn't any lead restriction back then. My buddy was shooting number 6 lead shot in his shotgun, and I was shooting number 4 copper shot in mine. We didn't know who killed the goose, so we flipped a coin and I won. I would take the goose home and have it for dinner that night.

We were checking hunters from shore and were going to go home at dark when we got a radio call about two waterfowl hunters shooting at some swans. We took the information and contacted the hunters as they were coming back to their car. The two juveniles had two swans. They said they thought the swans were snow geese, which were also white but half the size.

Since I lived the closest to the court, I issued the citations for hunting swan during the closed season and would have to appear in court the next day to file the affidavits. My buddy took my goose home with him. When he cleaned it, he found my copper shot and knew I was the one who killed it. He said it tasted real good, just the same as if he had killed it.

A small town north of Dayton on the Miami River had problems with their sewage treatment plant and permitted a large amount of raw sewage to run into the river. The sewage took all the oxygen out of the water and killed all the fish downstream for five miles. A fisherman noticed the dead fish and reported it to the region office.

I was assigned to investigate what caused the fish to die and find the party responsible. I took water samples above town and above and below every drainage pipe and ditch down to the dead fish. I also performed a dissolved-oxygen test on the samples and found no oxygen in the water below the sewage treatment plant. I sent the samples to the health department for a chemical analysis and assisted the fish biologist count and inventory all the dead fish. The city later paid for the dead fish.

Having to spend a lot of time working the deer season and chasing spotlighters in the southern part of the region, I slept many a night in my sleeping bag on the floor of the tool shop of the Tranquility Wildlife Area or had to drive a hundred plus miles back to my apartment and get home after 2:00 am.

I was still a hillbilly at heart and enjoyed working in the rolling hills where I grew up and didn't like working in the flat farm country up north. I still couldn't sell my house after a year of commuting, so I asked the regional supervisor if I could move down to the southern part of our region and fill the vacant wildlife agent position there. I was putting on a lot of miles driving down there to work all the time.

I told him I would rent my house in Lancaster and rent or buy a house in the region and move my family there. He finally said okay. I would work in the Adams, Brown, Clinton, and Greene Counties. My family was happy as we moved into Hillsboro, a small town seventeen miles from where we used to live in Greenfield. We bought a house and small barn on two acres at the edge of town. We had a garden, cats, chickens, pigeons, sheep, a rabbit, and a dog. It made the kids real happy, but now I had to cut two acres of grass and trim weeds on both of my days off.

My friend Bob would write me and kept telling me how great it was working in the state of Washington. One evening he called and said Washington was going to hire more wildlife agents and wanted me to take the test. The only catch was I had to do it in four days and didn't have time to prepare for it. I could go to the civil service office in Columbus and take the written test and then fly out for the oral interview later.

I had read a lot of stories about big-game hunting out west and had planned several hunting trips, but something would always come up and I would be unable to make the trip. I could hear the call, "Go west, young man." I thought if I passed the test and got hired, I could continue my wildlife law enforcement career in Washington and hunt big game whenever I wanted too. I didn't know anything about the Washington game laws, but I took the test anyway.

It took about a month for Washington to get back to me with my score. I needed a passing score of seventy, and I got a sixty-nine. They needed to hire twenty officers, so their personnel department called and said I could take the test again. I told them I wish they had called last week as I had just signed the papers on my second house. I would have to pass on the opportunity this time. They said they would be hiring again in 1971 and to reapply then.

Working down in Brown County along the Ohio River on a litter investigation, I found the name and address of a suspect who lived on a real bad country road. I had to drive across a small stream to get to his house. It had rained for the last two days, and the stream was real muddy and rising. I was working by myself, and halfway across the stream, my car started to float. I finally got across and was now wondering how I was going to get back to the main highway. I didn't want to have to spend the night with the person I just arrested for litter.

I contacted the suspect at his house as he couldn't drive across the stream in his old car to go to work. That was the filthiest, dirtiest house I have ever been in. There were chickens in the house walking on the kitchen table and roosting on the chairs and pooping all over the floor.

The floor didn't look like it had ever been scrubbed or cleaned in over a year. The suspect admitted dumping the litter because he didn't have time to take it to the county dump. I issued him a citation and left to drive back across the stream. I was not going to stay there, even if my car floated all the way down the stream to Cincinnati.

The next day, it was bright and sunny, and I had just come out of the prosecutor's office after filling the affidavit for litter in the court. I was walking back to my car when I heard a lady screaming, "He stole my baby! He stole my baby!" I saw a man running, carrying a young child in his arms, and a woman running after him, screaming, "He stole my baby!" I was standing there next to my car, in full uniform with a badge and wearing a sidearm, and the people were kinda looking at me like "Do something." I took off chasing the man with the child.

I caught the man in about a half block as he was just about to get into his car. I said, "Hold it."

He looked at me and at my badge, which said "Wildlife Agent," and said, "You can't arrest me."

I replied, "No, but you're not leaving until I find out what is going on here." The woman finally caught up to us and said, "He took my baby," and took the child out of his arms.

It appeared to be a domestic dispute with the man and woman fighting over custody of the child. A city police officer arrived, and I turned the man over to him. I was walking back to my car, and the people on the street were all slapping me on the back, thanking me and saying, "Boy, you sure can run." I was just glad the child was unhurt and safe.

There was a fish hatchery on Rocky Fork Lake, ten miles east of Hillsboro. They hatched muskellunge, a very large predatory fish called muskies, from eggs collected from other lakes throughout the state. After they hatched, the fry absorbed the egg sack, still attached to their body, in a couple days and were about three-fourths of an inch long and very hungry.

The hatchery manager would hatch carp eggs, which hatched in three days and were about one-fourth inch long, to feed to the Muskie fry.

The hatchery manager just had a bunch of Muskie eggs hatch and needed some carp fry to feed to the little muskies. A tub full of carp would produce over several million eggs, enough to feed all the little Muskie fry.

The hatchery manager asked the senior game protector, who lived close to the hatchery, and me to shoot some carp with our bows and arrows. We both had fishing licenses, and the carp were spawning in the shallow area of the lake. We could shoot them and take them back to the hatchery so the manager could collect the eggs and later we smoked the carp to eat. We shot a tubful of carp. Heck of a deal, getting paid for having fun.

When I would work with the game protectors, I would always let them have the first arrest because game protectors get kinda possessive of their patrol district and would call it "my county." They didn't like anyone else coming in and making a lot of arrests and making them look bad for not making the arrest themselves.

Somewhere in the back corner of my little brain, I could relate to thinking something like that when I was a game protector in Fairfield County. I told them they could make a lot more arrests if they were a little bit quieter along the creek walking up to the fishermen because they could hear them parting the bushes and rattling the leaves. I still made more arrests than the other officers as I would end up checking one more violator on the way home and making another arrest.

Sitting in the hills one afternoon, the week before squirrel season, I heard a .22 rifle shot. I parked my car above a house beside a block of timber where I heard the shot come from and put on my camo jacket over my uniform. I walked into the woods and waited near the house. Pretty soon I heard and saw two men carrying rifles and a gray squirrel walking toward the house. I contacted them and identified myself and said, "You're both under arrest." They both lived in the house, so I issued them each a citation for hunting squirrel during the closed season. I held the rifles and the squirrel for evidence and released them. They both forfeited $50 bail.

I was talking to my supervisor later that night, and he said he was so jealous because catching closed season squirrel hunters was a quality arrest with ODOW. I had caught six closed season squirrel hunters in the last year. That was more than the total caught by the other officers in the region. It seemed that I had a natural ability to be in the right spot at the right time.

A landowner down in Brown County called the region office and reported that his neighbor living in a trailer next door had killed a deer during the squirrel season. My supervisor and I met the local game protector and were going to contact the suspect. The suspect was not home, and we waited a half mile down the road by a woodlot until he returned. We could hear a lot of shooting, more than what was normal for squirrel hunting, about a mile south of us.

My supervisor decided he would drive down there and look around while I waited with the game protector in his car for our suspect to return. My supervisor called on his car radio and said there were four male subjects hunting rabbits and quail in the field in front of him. The season was closed, so he said he was going to walk out into the field and contact them. After about a half hour, my supervisor came back on the radio and said, "They got away." When they saw him in uniform, they took off running, and he couldn't catch them.

We were just starting to drive in his direction when four male subjects carrying shotguns walked up the road toward us. I got out and asked if they had any luck hunting. They said they only got one squirrel. We asked to check their hunting licenses and found it was the deer-poaching suspect and his three buddies. The one with the squirrel didn't have a hunting license, and they had fresh blood and rabbit hair in their hunting coat pockets. I called my supervisor on the radio and told him we had his four suspects in custody.

I asked them if they were the four hunters that ran away from my supervisor. They said no, they had been hunting squirrel. We separated them, and I was questioning the subject with the fresh blood in his coat pocket. He kept saying he was only hunting squirrel. He said his uncle got caught dynamiting fish down in Kentucky and his uncle had told him, "If you ever get caught, admit it and take your lumps."

My supervisor had found a car parked near the field, so we took the four suspects back there and right in the middle of the car rear bumper was a big round one-half-inch drop of fresh blood. I looked at the suspect and said, "Looks like you just got caught. Now start telling the truth."

I asked him to open the trunk of his car, and there lay three dead rabbits. They said the four of them had started out hunting squirrel in the afternoon, and as they were walking in the field heading back to the car, they jumped some quail and rabbits. They shot at the quail but didn't kill any. They jumped the rabbits and shot them and put them in the car and went back into the field to hunt the quail when they saw my supervisor.

We told them they would all be arrested for hunting rabbits during the closed season and that the one with the squirrel would also be charged with hunting squirrel without a license. We would take them to jail to post bail, and we could do it two ways: we could take them all in our cars and have their car towed, or we would take the deer-poaching suspect to jail in our car and hold identification from the other three and they could follow us to jail and save the expense of having the car towed.

They said they would follow us to jail. While my supervisor and I were driving to jail, we would question the deer-poacher suspect about killing the deer. The suspect was in the back seat of our car, and he kept denying killing any deer. It was now after dark, and I turned around and shined my flashlight on him and said, "You're lying. What did you do? Throw it away?"

He said, "Yeah."

I said, "Yeah what?"

He said, "I threw it away."

He said he was squirrel hunting in the woods behind his house and he fell asleep in the woods. He woke up, and a deer was standing about twenty yards from him eating acorns. So he shot it with his shotgun and killed it. He skinned the deer and put it in a sheet in the truck of his car and went to town and was going to give it to a friend. On the way to his friend's house, he stopped to see his wife in the hospital and stayed there for over an hour. It was over 90 degrees out, and when he came out, the deer had spoiled and smelled so bad he threw it away into the river.

At the jail I told him he would also be charged with killing a deer during the closed season since we had a witness to the violation. I let the game protector charge three of the hunters, and I filed the two charges on the deer poacher. All the subjects posted and later forfeited bail.

A landowner in Adams County called the game protector and reported coming in contact with two men shooting a deer during the closed season on his farm. He didn't know who they were, and they left before he could get their truck license number. They left the deer lying by the road. My supervisor and I drove down to help the game protector set up a stakeout on the deer in case the men came back to get it.

We hid our cars and were lying in the woods above the road near the dead deer, a big white-tailed buck. The carcass had the head cut off and was lying just inside the fence next to the road. Around 11:00 pm, a truck stopped by the fence at the exact location of the dead deer. I could read the license number and wrote it down, but I couldn't tell what state it was from as the numbers didn't match with Ohio plates. The truck left without anybody getting out.

After lying there for five hours, my supervisor and the game protector fell asleep and started to snore. I told them I didn't mind if we took turns sleeping for a while, but if the poachers were walking back down the road to get the deer, they would hear them snoring and we wouldn't catch the crooks. They just grumbled and went back to sleep and snoring. The truck never came back. I had to leave to be in court at 9:00 am, so I left at 6:00 am and headed home to change clothes and go to court.

I had just driven a mile up the road when I met a truck bearing a Texas license plate with the same number that I had written down earlier. We didn't have any portable radios back then, and I didn't have any way to warn my supervisor that the same truck was coming their way. If I turned around, they would have been too spooked to stop and pick up the deer.

Later that day I learned the truck stopped beside the dead deer and three men got out to pee. One said, "Hey, look what I found," and threw the deer head in the truck. They took off before my supervisor and the game protector could get out to the road and stop them. They were unable to catch up to the truck after they got back into their car, so they picked up the deer carcass.

That morning one of the poachers called the game protector's house and told the game protector's wife that they had found a deer head and wanted to keep it. The game protector's wife got the name and telephone number of the man, and my supervisor and the game protector contacted the suspect in town but were unable to obtain a confession about the poaching from him.

They seized the deer head. I took the carcass to the wildlife area and skinned it to look for bullets. It was shot twice with what appeared to be a 30-caliber bullet, but the bullets went through the carcass. The man moved back to Texas before I could question him and was never arrested.

I was working with the Adams County game protector in the same area one night, and about midnight, a car drove into a hayfield and a man sitting on the fender started shooting rabbits. We parked by the driveway into the field and blocked their escape route and waited for them to come out. We counted about twelve shots and figured we would have a couple of big charges to file on them for hunting after-hours. The car came to our location and I turned on the red light and it stopped.

An eighteen-year-old girl was driving the car, and her husband was the one doing the shooting. They only had three rabbits, and their six-month-old baby was lying on the back seat asleep. The man was charged with shooting rabbits after-hours. The girl was not charged for aiding and abetting in the violation.

Region 4 had a lot of poaching during the deer season, and they wanted officers from other regions to come over and help work spotlighters and to check hunters. My supervisor sent me and another new game protector over to work for three days. The next evening, around midnight, I was driving on one of the back roads to a poaching call with the new game protector. He said he used to live over there and knew the roads real well.

He wanted me to hurry up and get there. I was driving about fifty miles per hour and we came to a sharp corner and I was sliding around it and heading straight for a road sign. I had to do a lot of steering to get my car around that sign. I said, "I thought you knew this road." He said kinda sheepishly, "Well, I don't remember that corner." I slowed down the rest of the way.

My supervisor was working with me on the opening day of deer shotgun season down in Adams County. He was driving, so I could get out and do all the work checking the hunters. We saw a hunter without a license on his back come out of the woods with a double-barreled shotgun, and he took one look at our white patrol car bearing black state license plates with an eight-foot whip antenna and took off running. We chased him into a barn lot, and I jumped out in full uniform and took off running after him.

He was about five feet, five inches and having trouble getting across a barbed-wire fence next to a woodlot. I had closed the distance between him and me and was going to jump over the fence and grab him. He had just cleared the fence and I was about four feet from him when he turned around and pointed the shotgun at my belly and said, "Back up."

My service revolver was under my coat. I had no chance to draw it and I was too far away to grab the shotgun, so I very carefully assessed my situation. I identified myself and asked him, "Where are you going?" I told him I needed to check his hunting license and asked him to hand me the shotgun. He looked at me for what seemed like a long five minutes and I again said, "Hand me the shotgun." He handed me the shotgun and turned around to go back down into the woods.

I said, "Come on out of there. Let's go up to the car." He said he had to go to the bathroom, he had sh—t his pants! I wasn't nervous until I opened the shotgun and saw the double 00 buckshot in the right barrel and a slug in the left. Then my knees really started to shake. My boss said he thought I was going to die when the hunter pointed the gun at me.

We still were not issued handcuffs, so we put the violator between us in the front seat of the car and took him to jail. He smelled so bad we had to roll the windows down. The next day in court, the judge's brother, a lawyer, represented the violator, and he was found guilty and fined $20 for second-degree assault and hunting deer without a license. I guess you know what the judge thought a game warden's life was worth in Ohio back in 1969.

A man and his twenty-year-old son were setting muskrat traps during the closed season in a small stream in Highland County. The man, standing on the stream bank, was holding several traps and telling his son, standing in the water, where to put the unmarked traps in the stream bank. After I contacted them, I pulled several more of their unmarked traps that they had just set. I issued a citation to the son for trapping during the closed season and cited his father for aiding and abetting in the violation.

The son forfeited $50 bail, but the father came into court and told the judge that he was not trapping and didn't know the season was closed; he had just driven his son to the stream. I had already testified that the man had driven the car to the stream, had been holding unmarked traps, and had been giving instructions on where to place more traps. The judge said he didn't think the man was aiding his son and found him not guilty. That was only the second case I lost in six years, and I didn't like it any better than the first case.

It snowed about four inches in mid-January, and the Adams County game protector called me at the region office and wanted me to come and help him with a deer-poaching case. I had to drive over ninety miles and arrived about 1:00 pm and met him parked by a suspect's car. The game protector had caught a hound that came back to the car with the same name on its collar as the registered owner of the car.

We hid my car a mile down the road, and the game protector hid his car in a barn next to the suspect's car. I followed the footprints of two suspects and several dogs from the suspect's car into a field. My Polaroid camera would not take a photo of the shoe prints, so I drew a diagram of the two different shoe prints on a piece of paper. The two sets of prints separated after about thirty feet. I followed the footprints for about a half mile and found an empty 12-gauge double 00 shotshell lying on top of the snow and collected it for evidence.

The footprints continued on to a dead white-tailed doe deer and then met up again with the other set of footprints. They separated again after about thirty feet, and after another hundred yards, I found an empty 12-gauge slug shell casing on top of the snow next to the other set of shoe prints. The prints then lead to another dead doe about fifty yards away from the empty slug casing. It appeared as if the two suspects walked into the field and stood about one hundred yards apart and the dogs ran several deer past them and they both shot and each killed one doe.

After the suspects walked up to the dead deer, they walked up and over the hill following more deer tracks, maybe a buck. It was starting to get dark, so I returned to the suspect's car just as another car arrived. A man got out of the second car and got into the suspect's car, and then the second car drove away. I contacted the man in the suspect's car about the same time the game protector came out of the barn.

I was in uniform and advised the man we were investigating a deer-poaching complaint and advised him to get out of the car and produce some identification. The man started cursing and refused to get out of the car. I reached over and opened the driver's door and told him to get out. I stepped back and braced for a fight, but he just sat there and argued and wouldn't get out. I told him if he didn't get out, he would be arrested for obstructing. The man stepped out and was found to be the father of the owner of the car and the dogs.

The man said his son had just called him to pick up the car. He didn't know anything about deer poaching. He let us search the car, and we didn't find any more evidence of the violation. So we let him take it home. I had picked up the empty shell casings and took photos of the dead deer for evidence when I was in the field. The game protector said the suspect's family had been reported to poach deer. We were unable to make contact with the suspects that night.

We returned the next day and contacted the suspect and another man sitting in the suspect's car in town. I questioned them about what kind of shotguns they owned. The suspect said he didn't own a shotgun; he hunted with his dad's 12-gauge pump. He was lying about my other questions. He asked if he was under arrest, and I told him no. He opened the car door and got out and left. The other suspect said he owned a double-barrel 12-gauge. Neither of them would admit to shooting the dead deer and were not wearing shoes that matched the prints I saw in the field. I couldn't arrest them, so we left.

I sent the empty shotshell casings off to the Ohio Bureau of Criminal Investigation Lab for identification of the type of shotgun they were fired in. The lab reported that the slug casing was fired in a pump shotgun and the double 00 casing was fired in a single or double-barreled shotgun. I obtained descriptions and addresses of the two suspects' house and vehicles. I contacted the prosecutor in two different counties for search warrants for the shotguns and shoes that matched the diagrams I drew of the suspect's shoes prints in the field. That was the first search warrant I had ever applied for.

The game protector and I were able to find the double-barreled shotgun at the second suspect's house. The shotgun was seized and sent to the lab for tests, for comparison with the evidence shell casings. We were unable to find the other shotgun or any shoes similar to the prints I found in the field. The lab test came back positive for a match of the double-barreled shotgun and the evidence shell casing.

Suspect number 2 was charged by the prosecutor for shooting a deer during the closed season. The suspect came into court with the judge's brother for his attorney. I testified that the suspect stated he owned the double-barreled shotgun and nobody else had used it. The lab expert testified that the shotgun matched the evidence shell casing. The suspect also testified that he was the only one to use the shotgun. The Judge said,

"Well, just because a man owns a gun doesn't mean that he fired it," and found the suspect not guilty! I was upset at the time because I felt the judge and his attorney brother had a good thing going. Maybe it made me a better investigator.

I knew at the time a person could take plaster casts of the footprints, but I wasn't issued a kit and didn't have any plaster. I could have measured the prints for size and measured the length of the stride to give an indication of the size of the person. I could also have waited until later and maybe have caught the violators wearing the same boots or hunting with the pump shotgun. They say "patience brings rewards."

I could still hear a small voice say, "Go west, young man," when Bob Ford would write me a letter and tell me how good it was working for the game department in the state of Washington. I can remember the songs "Sitting on the Dock of the Bay" and "The Bluest Skies You Ever Seen Are in Seattle." I didn't know if that meant pretty blue or rainy blue.

I owned two houses at the time, but I made up my mind that if I sold one of them, I would take the test. My house was on the market for a year and the contract would be up in three days. I didn't have any offers on it, and I was discouraged and told my family I would give up my dream of moving west and remodel the house and live in Ohio. I tore off the back porch and was going to pour a concrete slab and build on a mudroom.

Coming home from work on the last day of the contract, my wife said, "Someone came today and bought the house." Now I had to pour a concrete slab and build the porch back on. I had never been west of the Mississippi; but if I passed the test, we would pack up and move to Washington, and I would continue my wildlife law enforcement career in the Pacific Northwest.

Bob sent me a copy of the Washington Game Code, fishing and hunting regulations, and a copy of the commercial fishing regulations to study. I never would have guessed what a "clam gun" was or how to cook a "geoduck." Living in mid-America, it was hard for me to visualize the ocean tide's going up and down twice a day.

After selling our house, we house-sat a small house on Rocky Fork Lake for a friend while they stayed in Arizona for the winter and stored our furniture in his garage. I took the test for a wildlife agent position in the state of Washington again at the civil service office in Columbus. I went to the library and found a book about the state of Washington. It was printed in 1940, but it described things about Washington I didn't know.

I had another long wait until I learned if I passed or if I would have to buy another house and stay there. After I found out I passed the test, I flew out to Washington for the oral interview. My friend Bob met me at the airport and drove me to Olympia for the oral exam. One of the interviewers asked me when I was going back, and I misunderstood him to be asking, "When are you coming back?" I replied, "The first of July when you hire me." We all had a good laugh.

Bob took me over to his house in Eastern Washington to see what it looked like. The wind was always blowing in Ellensburg, and I didn't think it was as pretty as Western Washington. I really liked Mount Rainier and the snowcapped Cascade Mountains in May. There were no Mexican restaurants in the small towns where I lived; so when Bob asked if I wanted tacos for dinner, I asked, "Is that a drink?"

After the interview, I had another long wait until I learned if I passed the oral interview and would get hired. My buddy in Ohio said there was a rumor that someone was moving out to the state of Washington. Washington and wondered if it was me. I didn't deny it. I just said, "It must be you, and you are trying to throw suspicion on everyone else." Well, I finally found out I scored 97.3 on the oral and would start July 1.

The State of Washington Personnel Department must have called the Columbus office for a background check on me because the regional supervisor came to see me and asked what was going on. I told him I was going to move to the state of Washington to be a wildlife agent for the game department. He said he hated to see me leave.

I went to the division office in Columbus, just before I left, to say goodbye to friends and thanked John Adams for helping me get hired. The assistant chief of enforcement said, "Bud, I can see you now, running across the mountains with an Indian woman hot on your heels, chasing you with a big club." We all laughed, and I left, not knowing that would almost come true that winter.

I quit the Ohio Division of Wildlife in mid-June, stored our furniture in my mother-in-law's barn, took my two weeks' paid vacation, and headed out west for a new adventure. I rented a car top carrier from U-Haul and loaded my car with things I would need for the next three months of training school. I must have overloaded my car as the radiator kept overheating going through the Badlands and the Rocky Mountains.

Gas prices were about eighteen to twenty cents per gallon, and I was mad when I had to pay twenty-five cents a gallon in Yellowstone Park. Those "good old days" gas prices are long gone!

MOVING WEST

On June 27, 1971, we drove across the state line into the town of Clarkston in Southeastern Washington. It didn't look anything close to what the 1940 book described. I started to wonder if the rest of the state would be different too. I planned to drive around the state and see what it looked like before we arrived in Olympia to see where I would like to live and work in the future.

On our way to Olympia, I stopped in to visit my friend Bob in Ellensburg. It was a nice college town; but the wind was still blowing and would blow dirt in my mouth, and the trees grew in a leaning position. I didn't think I would want to live there. I was so surprised at the clean water in the streams and rivers.

I almost wanted to stop and run out into them and take a drink. The streams and rivers in Ohio were always muddy, and some in the summer would turn black. The cities would take water out of the river, upstream of the city, and discharge sewage-treated water downstream. Some streams in Southern Ohio would also be a rusty brown from strip mine acid runoff.

Training school for the Washington Game Department (WGD) in Olympia, Washington, would start on July 1 for me, along with thirty other cadets, at the Saint Martin's College. There were two cadets to a room and four rooms to a dorm, with a large seating area in the middle. This is where we held most of our training classes. When the training officers introduced themselves and me to the other new hires, they said, "You want to watch out for Holste. He doesn't drink."

I soon found out that the beer flowed pretty freely at night in the dorm and after field-training exercises. One of the training officers wanted me to be his chauffer since I didn't drink. About halfway through training, I rode back to the dorm one night with three other cadets that I hung around with and left the training officer with his drinking buddies. I thought he might try and get me fired for leaving him there, but he didn't. He was a good officer when he was working in the field.

The administration and divisions were similar to Ohio with chiefs for each division and ten regional offices in different locations throughout the state, but the field officers were called wildlife agents. The training was about the same as it was back in 1965. Division personnel and other officers would train us on department policy; fishing and hunting regulations; search, seizure, and arrest authority; and first aid.

The other division chiefs would ask where I went to college, and I would tell them I graduated from the school of hard knocks. I didn't go to college; I traded my six and a half years of law enforcement experience for the two-year college requirement. They would kinda turn up their noses and say, "Oh," and leave.

The game department contracted with the state patrol for use of their car radio system. Except for remote mountainous patrol areas, it was nice to know that if you needed help at night, all you had to do was just call on the radio. Someone would be there 24-7.

One of the older officers (Norm) was giving us training on searching a car and wanted me to pretend I was the violator. I sat on a chair, a make-believe car. Norm was going to show the other cadets how to get me out of the car and search it. Having checked a lot of violators in Ohio and since I didn't just fall off the turnip wagon yesterday, I pretended I wouldn't roll down my window to talk to him. Norm almost got mad and said, "Roll down your window!"

It got a laugh from the rest of the cadets, so I finally got out of the make-believe car. Norm was talking to the other cadets and wasn't watching me as he showed them how to search the car, so I just walked away and hid. Norm turned around with a surprised look when he saw I was gone, and the whole class just busted out laughing. I came back and told them that you always want to control the suspect or violator. Maybe they learned a good lesson that would help them in the future.

The state patrol was going to teach us pistol marksmanship, and I told the instructor that I was a certified NRA firearms instructor and held a master rating. I suggested he help some of the new cadets that had never shot a pistol very much. We were all standing on the seven-yard line, and he told us to load our pistols. I had practiced this over a thousand times while shooting combat competition and loaded in a few seconds and holstered my pistol and was standing ready to fire.

The instructor came up to me and told me to go ahead and load my pistol. I told him I already did. He said, "No, you didn't," so I opened my pistol and showed him the live cartridges in it. We were then instructed to pull out our pistol and take our time and shoot six rounds at the head on the silhouette target. This was too easy.

In past competition events, I would shoot twelve rounds, including a reload, from the hip in less than twenty-five seconds from this same distance and have a near perfect score 99 percent of the time. I took out my pistol and shot all six rounds in a small hole the size of a nickel into the head of the target so it looked like it had a left eye.

The other cadets had holes scattered all over their targets. The instructor looked at my target and asked, "Where are the rest of the rounds?" I said they were all in that same hole. I told him again that I had a master rating and shot competition. We then shot sixty rounds for qualification, and I shot the center out of my target and impressed the other cadets.

The patrol let us drive some of their old cars and taught us defensive driving. We had to drive thirty-five miles per hour at the instructor, and then he would give a signal with his arm to go right or left. We then had to stop in front of an orange plastic cone. Nobody hit him. We had to drive as fast as we could between and around six cones in a line and then back up around all the cones and stop in front of another cone. The instructor tried but couldn't beat my time.

The last week of school, we had night-patrol training. Two cadets were paired up with two wildlife agents, and since we were not commissioned, we were instructed not to do anything but just observe and learn. After dark, we were following a car with two men that were spotlighting a field when the passenger stuck a .22 rifle out the window and shot.

I didn't see anything in the field for him to shoot at, and since I had six and a half years' experience working spotlighters, I knew something wasn't right when the four seasoned game wardens couldn't contain two would-be poachers after the stop.

One of the poachers was about to walk past me and leave the area, so I grabbed him by the arm and said, "Get back here." He jerked back, and I ripped his coat sleeve off. He acted real mad. A little later, he was running away from the training officers, and they said, "Bud, get him." I caught him and put an arm lock on him and threw him on the ground. They then told me to search the car, and I found some federal license plates.

I was having too much fun, so they told me and another cadet to go search the field for the phantom deer. The other cadet was real excited and believed this was a real poaching case. We couldn't find any deer, and I told him I was going to holler, "Here it is," and see what happened. I was getting paid for having fun, so I didn't. One of the suspects was wearing a wig, and it kept falling off his head. I recognized him, a USFW officer, but couldn't remember his name.

When we were driving back to town, our training officers asked the other cadet and me, "What do you think about working night patrol?" The other cadet thought it was the real thing. I told them it wasn't real because I recognized one of the poachers and they hadn't shot at anything. We all went back to the department warehouse, and all the cadets were wide-eyed and excited, claiming they all caught some poachers too.

I said, "You guys are crazy. This was a setup deal." It was. The men playing the poachers were federal fish and wildlife agents. The one that I ripped the coat sleeve off of said, "Boy, you just about broke my arm when you had me on the ground."

There were ten regions in the state, five on the east side and five on the west side of the Cascade Mountains. The training officer told us where all the vacant patrol stations were and then talked to us one at a time and asked where we wanted to work. I told them I would like to work in the small town of Wenatchee because it had a lot of fishing and hunting. I was six foot three and two hundred pounds, and the training officer said, "No, you're too big. You're going to Seattle in region 7." The officer that just left there was small, and he had a lot of problems.

I was pretty bummed out when he said I was going to be stationed in the big city of Seattle. There were two stations open, one in the north end and another one in the south end. I asked which one was the best, and he said the north station. I said, "I'll take it." It was a blessing in disguise; nobody knew when I was on a day off, and people would call the region office about nuisance wildlife.

There wasn't any deer or elk damage, so I could work a lot of investigations and make a lot of arrests. Having been raised on a farm with a steady diet of meat, potatoes, gravy, and vegetables, I soon adapted to and enjoyed eating crab, scallops, oysters, and fish from Puget Sound on a regular basis.

It was kind of ironic because all during cadet school, there was a game warden advertisement on the radio: "Want to be a game warden, live in the mountains by a stream, and breathe clean, fresh air every day? Call

@#$%&*# today." After working in and around Columbus, Cincinnati, and Dayton—big cities in Ohio—I ended up in the biggest city in the state of Washington. At least there was only about one-third of the population of Ohio and twice the landmass.

My neighbor was over at my house one day and asked, "What does a game warden do in Seattle?" I told her I arrested illegal fishermen on Lake Washington and that a lot of poacher's fish and hunt all over the state and bring the illegal wildlife back to Seattle and I arrest them and make a lot of arrests. She just said, "Oh."

After completing the training, I felt like the WGD was about thirty years behind times in their laws, policies, vehicles, and operating procedures. They had a very loose chain of evidence with confiscated firearms and meat. The old films I used to show at sport club meetings had late forties and early fifties vintage cars in them and would always break.

The game department issued a little more equipment than Ohio, but they still bought cars without air-conditioning for us to drive. No four-wheel-drive trucks to drive in the mountains or to haul big game like elk and moose. The uniform had a department patch, with a deer, duck, and fish on the left shoulder and a Red Cross patch on the right. The violators would see the Red Cross patch and say, "You don't have authority to arrest me," and it caused a lot of confrontations.

The uniform policy required a tie to be worn with the longsleeve shirt. The standard issue long black tie had to be hand tied and was a very dangerous thing to have around one's neck when fighting or struggling with an offender. Ohio issued a clip-on tie, but it was green. I told the uniform supply officer it was a safety issue and asked if he would order me a clip-on tie. He said he would after the last shipment was all gone.

That would take about three years, so I took an Ohio tie apart and made my own. I had to cut about a foot of material out of the center of the black tie, sew it back together, and retie it. I would carry it in my jockey box in the car to put it on when my supervisor showed up unexpectedly or when going to club meetings or attending court.

In addition to the uniform, binoculars, a flashlight, and an old wooden boat, they did issue a first-aid kit, a canvas tarp, snowshoes, a shovel, mud and snow tires and chains, and a tow chain. They purchased a fleet of 1971 Nash Ramblers "Matadors" for all the new officers to drive. They didn't hold up very well on the rough country roads. I had to have new transmissions put in mine four times. Every time I got stuck in the mud or snow and spun my wheels a little, the transmission burned out.

The warehouse would install an old Army blackout running light on the front bumper, with a switch under the dash, for us to use to follow poachers at night. They also installed a cutout switch to shut off our taillights so when we followed poachers at night in the dark and hit our brakes, they wouldn't light up the whole countryside and alert the poachers.

The fish hatcheries had sleeping bunks and a kitchen area built into them for personnel to stay at during training or extended patrols. There were also patrol cabins built or leased from the forest service in remote areas for the officers to stay in. We had a per diem allowance, and if we worked over twelve hours, we could claim two meals for that day. The officers could also buy food, "camp groceries," on state vouchers to eat while staying at the cabins on extended patrols. Most were too far away from fast-food restaurants.

The training officer told me that back in the forties when he started to work, he had to drive his own car and officers were paid mileage but nothing for meals. He and another officer were working down on the Columbia River on a floating patrol. They slept under the bridge in their car, and they didn't have any money left for food. The one officer took off his uniform shirt, and the other officer put an old pair of handcuffs on him.

They pulled into a café along the road, and the officer wearing the uniform told the cook he was taking a prisoner to jail and ordered a meal for both of them. The officer in handcuffs started complaining he couldn't eat with the cuffs on. He said he would be good if he could have the cuffs off while he ate his meal. So the cuffs were taken off.

When they were just about done eating, the officer without the shirt ran out the door, pretending to get away. The officer with the shirt pretended to chase him out into the parking lot and then they jumped into the car and took off without paying for the meal. No wonder the old-time game wardens had a bad reputation with the public.

The game department enforced title RCW 77 and WAC 232 rules and regulations. The misdemeanor violations had a fine of up to $500 with thirty to ninety days in jail with a standard $25 bail. The gross misdemeanor violations were punishable with one-year jail time and up to a $1,000 fine. Standard bail was $350.

In Washington, the officers were issued a citation book that had a space to write out a valid violation charge so the officer didn't have to file an affidavit in court later. The citations were sent or taken into court on the next working day. The citation book was about three inches by eight inches and would fit in the hip pocket real good. Then we were issued an aluminum box to hold and cover the citation book and it wouldn't fit into our pocket, making it necessary to carry it in one hand and making it awkward to hold while looking through binoculars. The fishing pamphlet only had about forty pages, and it had our names and telephone number in it. It was also small enough to fit into the back pants pocket. There were so many regulations it was easier than it was in Ohio to arrest the fishermen for something.

The hunting pamphlet was a twenty-by-thirty-two-inch piece of paper with the regulations and a map of the hunting units printed on both sides. It would fold down to four by eight inches but was pretty cumbersome trying to read and handle in the car. I would cut it along the folds and staple it back together like a book. I could read it from front to back when people asked me questions I had to look up. The hunting units were on the back, and I would have to open another pamphlet to look up a unit description.

My first day on the job, I was given a Seattle City map and a county map as most of my patrol district encompassed the northern part of King County. I still had to be self-motivated. I was told to contact the officer in the next patrol district. He would introduce me to the local law enforcement agencies and courts and show me around my patrol district.

I met wildlife agent Larry Kerr, who lived twenty miles away in the small town of Carnation. We would work together a lot. We both liked to fish and hunt and became good friends. He was twenty years older than me and soon became a father figure to me. The first day we patrolled the Snoqualmie River for fishermen, I told him to stop and said we should check a couple likely suspects.

We would arrest them and drive on, and I would tell him to stop again and then arrested a couple more violators. Larry would ask me, "How did you know they didn't have a license?" I told him they just looked guilty. I told him, "We are not 'windshield' game wardens. We have to stop and get out of the car and check people. A lot of them don't have licenses."

The next night, we worked spotlighters in the 180,000-acre Weyerhaeuser tree farm and observed two men in a truck shining a light around the clear-cut. The driver was shining the light, and the passenger was standing in the open truck bed and pointing a rifle over the cab of the truck.

The rifle was still loaded when we stopped them, and they were arrested for hunting with the aid of an artificial light during the closed season and possession of a loaded firearm in a motor vehicle (LGMV). Both were later found guilty in court and paid a $350 fine, and the rifle was confiscated. The other new cadets couldn't believe my luck at making arrests.

We hiked into a high lake—this was a first for me—to check fishermen. There weren't any fishermen at the lake, and Larry just happened to have a fishing pole along. He said he had to test the lake and see if it had any fish in it and report his findings back to the fish biologist. I was still a nonresident and hadn't bought a license yet to test it, so I carved my initials into a three-foot-in-diameter log next to the spillway. A fish biologist found the log with my name still there twenty years later.

In October, I had lived in Washington long enough to be a resident and bought a fishing and hunting license. I had shot crippled and injured deer that were hit by vehicles in Ohio but never shot a deer to put in my freezer. Larry took me deer hunting the day before my thirty-first birthday, and I shot my first deer, a fat two-point buck. That was the start of our hunting together. Larry and I would hunt bear, deer, elk, and turkeys many times after that.

The department didn't provide a sidearm, but we could carry our own if it was covered by our coat. They wanted us to take it off when we went into stores to check license dealers, go in a restaurant to eat, or attended club meetings. I bought a model 10 Smith & Wesson .38 special from Larry for $25 with a holster. It was light, easy to carry, and accurate.

I was getting into my car in Downtown Seattle, after checking a taxidermy shop, when a man who worked for National Marine Fisheries showed me his badge and asked, "You're an officer. You wearing a gun?" I replied yes. He said a Seattle police officer was requesting backup on a "shots fired" call and said, "Come with me." We drew our pistols and went into a café following the police officer. We didn't find anyone. I started carrying my revolver all the time after that.

There were four sportsmen clubs that I attended on a monthly basis: the Western Bass Club, the Kenmore Big Game Club, the Bothell Sportsmen, and the Snoqualmie Valley Bear Hunters Club. The sportsmen knew I carried a sidearm when I was in the field checking them, so in the summer, I didn't try to cover it with a coat. I wouldn't wear it when I presented a program to the lower grades in schools as the little kids would keep asking over and over again, "Why do you carry a gun?"

I did such a good job presenting career day programs to the schools that the principal gave my name to every school district in Seattle, and I almost had a full-time job just doing that. I only put on one radio program where the people could call in and ask questions. It was after the bars opened at night; a few drunks would call in, and it was a waste of my time.

The game department would hold a check station at a wide spot of a four-way intersection on the Weyerhaeuser tree farm. The officers would check fish and wildlife harvested and licenses. I was assigned to work there on the opening weekend of deer season and checked over five hundred hunters. I wrote seventeen citations for failing to tag their deer, no license, loaded firearm in a motor vehicle, and possession of protected wildlife.

It was fun, but all the hunters would ask me "Where are all the deer?" every time they would pull up to the intersection. After a while I would ask them first, "Who shot the deer?" just to get a reaction out of them. A few would look stunned and start to stutter and say, "I did" and then try to put their unnotched tag on the deer.

One hunter lived nearby and figured he would come back and shoot another deer another day. About 10:00 am one morning, I heard a shot up the road from our check station. A short time later, a truck came around the bend in the road and stopped when they saw the department check station sign. I motioned for them to come ahead to me.

I could see both lever-action rifles had cartridges in them and asked, "Who shot the deer?" The passenger started to stutter and said, "I did. It's in the back. It's a doe, and it's in the toolbox!" I asked them both to step out of the truck, and I unloaded their rifles.

I looked in the toolbox in the bed of the truck and found a dead blacktail doe deer.

He said they didn't see any deer all morning and were going home when they saw the doe, so they shot it. They threw it in the box without gutting it because another hunter was coming down the road. Both hunters were cited for possession LGMV and taking a doe deer during the closed season. Both forfeited $375 in court later.

A man driving a Ford Bronco pulled up to the check station. His wife, wearing a dress and holding a small baby, was sitting in the passenger seat next to him. A little four-year-old boy in the back seat stuck his head out of the window and said, "Daddy shot a deer!" That reminded me of my poaching years and my boy. The man got a sick look on his face when I looked into the back of the Bronco and saw the small two-point blacktail buck with a deer tag attached to one of the antlers.

Upon checking the man's hunting license, I found he still had an unnotched deer tag in his billfold and his wife's deer tag was on the dead deer. I looked her in the eye and said, "You didn't shoot that deer, did you? She said no. I arrested the husband for failing to notch his tag. He forfeited $25 bail. I couldn't believe with all the fish and wildlife in Washington that people would try and cheat so bad.

Since I didn't have an elk season in my patrol district, I was assigned to go work in another region on opening day. I had never checked an elk hunter before and didn't know about all the party hunting that went on in the hunting camps. I was given a road map and court information and assigned to work in the Quinault Rain Forest. I stayed at a small motel with a leaking roof in a very small town and ate my meals in the local café. The first hunter I checked didn't have a license.

I could hear a lot of shooting coming from far away up the canyon and drove in that direction. I contacted two hunters carrying out large bags of boned-out elk meat, which they said belonged to another hunter. They didn't have any information from him regarding the elk head or his elk tag number. They said the local game warden said they could do that, so I took their name and address and let them go. I gave the info to the local officer.

It rained over seven inches one day, and the hunters would all grumble when I asked to check their hunting license, which was buried under several layers of clothes under their raincoat. I found an illegal cow elk head lying beside the road and a group of hunters pulling a U-Haul trailer full of game bags of boned-out meat. They had three spike elk heads in the trailer and said all the meat came from those three elk. I was so inexperienced in the ways of the elk hunters I let them go. I shudder to think how many poachers beat me that first year.

I received a radio call late in the afternoon about an illegal cow elk that had been shot and partly skinned. I found the cow and found that someone had started skinning the hind legs. The poacher must have been interrupted by the reporting party and took off. I went back to town and ate dinner at the café and then parked my car in front of the motel so the hunters would think I was there.

I put on a red wool hunting jacket over my uniform and walked back to the kill site. If the poacher saw my car in town, they might come back and take part of the meat. About halfway to the kill site, a car was coming up the road behind me, so I jumped into the ditch behind a tree.

There was a sixteen-inch log lying beside the road, and after the car went by, I grunted and strained to roll it across the road so the car would have to stop on the way back.

I waited on the hillside above the log for an hour until the car returned and stopped in front of the log. I was stepping down to the road and misjudged the distance in the dark and fell hard on my left knee. It was really hurting, but I hobbled up to the car and open the car door and said, "State wildlife agent." There were three men in the car, and they jumped out fighting mad. I asked them if they were camping up the road, and they said no.

They had been drinking pretty heavy and objected to me stopping them. I advised them that I was investigating an illegal elk kill and wondered why they would be on this forest service road so late at night. I had showed them my uniform when they got out, but they were cursing and didn't believe I was an officer and wanted to see my identification card.

They acted like they were going to start a fight with me, so I pulled my jacket back to get my billfold out with my picture and identification card. I was so nervous I dropped it on the ground. They saw my holster with my sidearm under my jacket and settled down and let me look into the trunk of their car. They didn't have any meat. One of them helped me push the log off the road, and then they left.

I was working all by myself and didn't have a portable radio to maintain contact with other officers and decided this was not very smart and walked back to the motel and went to bed. The local officer checked the three men hunting the next day and they told him they thought another officer had been standing in the bushes as they didn't think I could have pushed the log across the road by myself. I made ten arrests that week, which was as many as the rest of the officers made in the region.

The game department had jurisdiction over game fish and game animals. The steelhead trout is a sea-run rainbow trout that is classified as a game fish and can only be taken with a hook and line.

In 1853, Washington was created a new territory by President Franklin Pierce, and he appointed governor Isaac L. Stevens to negotiate a treaty with the Indian tribes. In general, the treaties called for the end of tribal warfare (and are therefore considered peace treaties), the surrender of vast amounts of Indian lands to the United States government, and the confinement of the tribes to several small reservations.

The wording of the Stevens treaties stated, "The right of taking fish, at all usual and accustomed grounds and stations, is further secured to said Indians in common with all citizens of the territory, and of erecting temporary house for the purpose of curing them, together with the privileges of hunting, gathering roots and berries, and pasturing their horses on open and unclaimed land."

Some of the tribes didn't sign the treaties and would set gill nets for salmon and steelhead in the rivers off the reservation. The department of fisheries had jurisdiction over the salmon and would pull the nets and arrest the Indians for the violations.

Over the next several years, the game department and the Indian tribes would have disagreements over the netting of the steelhead, even to the extent of physical fights and gunfire during the confrontations. The department's tactical squad and a group of wildlife agents were called into the office in Olympia on the third of January in 1972 and were instructed to pull the illegal nets in the Nisqually River east of Olympia.

I was assigned, along with two other new cadets—Ralph, a wildlife agent, and Jim, a fish biologist—to stand guard at the bridge over the Nisqually River to prevent the tribal members from dropping rocks on the officers pulling nets into the patrol boats. The other two officers were disappointed as they thought they would miss out on all the action.

We secured the bridge and directed car traffic until the patrol boats passed under the bridge and headed upstream. The officers in the patrol boats had arrested two male Indian subjects and pulled their nets and seized their boat. The officers pulled into shore above the bridge, and the tactical squad and all the other officers came and discussed the next plan of attack.

The boat patrol officers transferred the prisoners and the boat with the net over to the three of us new officers, and everybody left to go upstream and pull more nets. We were instructed to hold the two prisoners until a sheriff car came to transport them to jail. Having seven years of law enforcement experience, I knew this was very poor planning by the department administrators.

About ten minutes after all the other officers left, an old Indian man and woman, about seventy years old, arrived and started arguing and cursing us. Then two young Indian females about eighteen came and started arguing and spitting on us. I got on the radio and asked the regional agent in charge of the operation when the sheriff's car would be there as we were getting outnumbered.

We didn't have the prisoners handcuffed, but they just stood there by my patrol car without resistance. I don't know why they didn't try to get away as there were six of them against Ralph and me. Jim was holding the boat with the net down by the river. The sheriff car finally arrived just as two more Indian males about twenty years old came up and headed for the officer holding the boat.

The two latest arrivals tried to get the boat away from Jim. I told Ralph to go help Jim by the river. I searched the two prisoners and pushed them into the back of the sheriff's car and told him to take them to jail just as the last two male subjects started physically fighting with Jim and

Ralph.

I ran down to the river and grabbed the closest subject fighting with Ralph and threw him on the ground and held him there with an arm lock. I told Ralph to help Jim hold the boat and not to let the evidence get taken away. The old Indian woman walked up to me and was going to hit me on the head with a very large stick.

The old wildlife agent, Norm, who gave us the training on searching a car that I had made a fool of during cadet training, showed up and said to the old woman, "If you hit him, I will hit you."

I said, "No, Norm, don't let her hit me. Just keep her away from me." The other Indian male fighting with Ralph finally broke loose and tried to run away just as more officers arrived. They had him surrounded, and he ran toward the river trying to get away.

The old man and the old woman started yelling at him to jump in the river and get away. It was winter and very cold out and the young fighter didn't want to jump into the water. They kept yelling at him to jump in and get away. The officers were closing in on him, so he jumped into the river and tried to swim to the other shore—a very bad mistake.

The cold water took all the energy out of him, and I thought he was going to drown. The patrol boat came down the river and picked him up. The two male subjects were arrested for obstructing and assault and booked into jail. I asked Ralph and Jim if they had enough excitement, and they said yes. Everybody learned a good lesson in arrest and seizure that day.

A few months later, we were going to pull more nets from the river with the Thurston County Sheriff Department coming along to transport prisoners. Five wildlife agents, two deputies, and I would ride in a sheriff's van into Franks Landing on the reservation to secure the riverbank. To keep tribal members from throwing rocks at the patrol officers' boat coming up the river to pull nets. We just pulled into the group of houses and stepped out of the van and were immediately surrounded by about twenty-five adult tribal members, men and women.

They demanded to know what we were doing there. They were advised we were going to secure the riverbank to prevent any violence to our officers coming upstream in boats. Several males displayed knives and made verbal threats. Then the group all ran back behind the house as fast as they arrived.

Before we could secure the riverbank, the group came running back around the house, picking up sticks and two-by-fours and breaking them into clubs and heading our way. That was the first time in my short career when I thought I was going to have to shoot someone. I wasn't about to let one of them cut me or beat on me or on another officer with a two-by-four. I just hoped it wouldn't be a woman. The group turned before reaching us and ran to their cars and drove up the river.

After the patrol boats passed, we received a call from the officers upriver at the handicap boat launch requesting assistance. The twenty-five tribal members had arrived there and were obstructing the patrol boats from landing with nets and prisoners. We arrived and got between the patrol boats and the tribal members and instructed them to stay back. One Indian male stood in front of me and was pushing back on the boat I was trying to secure.

I told him to let go or he would be arrested. He kept pushing, and I turned to the officer behind me and said, "I am taking him down." I put a headlock on the subject and pushed him to the ground. The other officer helped me secure his arms, and we placed the subject next to the van. I think the subject's nose got bloodied when he was held up to the van and searched. He was from a South Dakota tribe and didn't even live in Washington.

After the event was over, all the officers met with the director and the chief of enforcement in the warehouse to discuss the arrests and operation. They asked the officers what we thought of the operation. When it was my turn, I told them that the officers should be provided more protection: with Mace spray, batons, handcuffs, and bulletproof vests. They never provide any.

Larry called me one night and wanted me to help him with a report of a deer killed by a local farmer's son during the closed season. The next morning, we drove to a dairy farm along the Snoqualmie River and contacted the boy's mother, and she said he was in the barn feeding the cows. It had rained a lot, and the barn lot was a real muddy mess and smelled pretty bad.

We were talking to the suspect in the barn, and he was denying killing any deer when I happened to look up into the rafters. A skinned-out carcass of a deer was hanging from the rafters over a muddy area where the cow and flies rested during the day. That was the worst place a person would want meat hanging to eat on his table. With the flies and the stink, I don't know how they could have eaten any of it. The suspect was arrested for killing a deer during the closed season. He later forfeited $350 in court.

Having grown up in the Midwest where it would rain several inches at a time in a downpour, I had the tendency to want to quit working when it started to rain and go home for the day. I soon realized it would only rain a quarter of an inch after a whole day of raining. The fishermen and hunters would just put on a raincoat and continue to recreate, so I would continue to work and put on my raincoat, too, and check them.

I couldn't believe all the calls I received from other officers with bits of information about violations in their patrol district. They would want me to contact someone and investigate the violation. A wildlife officer from Oregon called and wanted me to contact a man living in a town near me after someone got the license number of the truck with suspects spotlighting elk. The truck had a Washington license, and he didn't want to drive up without more information.

The next morning, at 6:00 am, I went to contact the suspect at his house. The wife of the suspect was up when I knocked on the door. I introduced myself and asked if I could speak with her husband. She went into the bedroom and came back out and sat on the couch and just stared at me. After about ten minutes, I asked her if her husband was getting up. She said, "I think you want to see me." I was a little confused.

I told her I was investigating a poaching complaint for Oregon, and she said she was the one driving the truck, not her husband. She had been down visiting her two sons who lived near Portland, and they wanted to go spotlighting for elk. They spotlighted a bull elk. The bull elk just stood there, so one of her sons shot it. They were loading it in the truck when someone came by and got the license number. The meat was in Oregon. I obtained a written statement, and her sons were arrested by the Oregon officer.

I almost went into shock on opening day of fishing season. It was like a zoo with all the fishermen and boats on all the lakes. In Ohio, fishing season was open all year, and a person could use two fishing poles, set three lines across a stream with fifty hooks each, and set fifty bank lines on poles or tree limbs. Only during the warm summer would there be more than a hundred fishermen on any one lake.

In Washington, the fishermen could only use one pole. Every lake had boats with at least three fishermen in them, spaced about twenty-five feet apart and getting their lines tangled with one another's. I checked the first lake and arrested several fishermen for fishing without a license and left.

The chief of enforcement, Walter Neubrech, came up from

Olympia and rode with me later that day while we checked more fishermen. He knew my arrest record and thought I was doing a good job. I was one of six officers who wrote over 125 tickets that year. Apparently, some of the other administrators didn't think I would make it past probation. The chief said he wanted to call them all together and tell them, "I told you so." I thanked him for taking a chance and hiring me.

There were a lot of small lakes in my patrol district, and I would arrest a lot of fishermen on Green Lake in Seattle. They would come to court and plead guilty. The judge would dismiss the charge and find them not guilty but made them pay $4 court cost. The dismissals made my conviction percentage rate change, and I was getting very discouraged.

One day it was cool and I had a wool shirt over my uniform and I contacted two men fishing on Green Lake. One subject didn't have a license and wouldn't provide me with any identification. I told him he was under arrest and I was taking him up to my patrol car parked on the street. I held onto the violator, only five foot three, by his left arm with my right hand and held his fishing pole in my left hand.

His buddy, five foot ten and 250 pounds, came up behind me and started arguing; and I told him to leave me alone or he would be arrested for obstructing. The next thing I knew, the violator hit me in the left eye with his right fist and his buddy jumped on my back and knocked me down. The violator ran away when I turned to defend myself from his buddy.

I arrested my attacker for obstructing, and we walked to my car without another incident. I called radio dispatch on my car radio for a Seattle police officer for backup and to assist in transporting my prisoner to jail. My attacker, a longshoreman, was so big and muscular we couldn't get the handcuffs on his arms behind his back when the officer arrived to transport him.

A woman came up to me when I went back down to the lake to pick up the suspects' fishing pole. The woman asked, "Are you an officer?" I said yes. She said, "I got the license number of the car of the man who ran away." I thanked her and took her name and address. At least some people like law enforcement.

I ran the registration of the car license number provided me and contacted the suspect at his home and issued him a citation for fishing without a license and assault. Both violators came into court with an attorney and appeared before the same judge that would dismiss all my fishing cases.

The prosecutor was taking my testimony on the witness stand, and the defense attorney started arguing about my authority to arrest anyone for assault and objected to my testimony. The judge told the court clerk to strike out my testimony from the court record. The prosecutor started arguing with the judge and the judge said, "Cases dismissed."

I told my supervisory about the judge and all the dismissals, and we went in to meet with the judge. I asked the judge if he didn't like the game department, me, or the way I testified. The judge said, "No, you're a good officer, and your testimony is real good."

I asked the judge, "Then why did you dismiss those cases for assault?"

The judge said, "Well, you saw how that prosecutor was acting. He made me look like a fool. I had to set him in his place."

I told the judge, "Well, you made me look like a fool, and I also got a black eye out of the deal." The judge said he was sorry. I asked the judge why he had dismissed the other twenty-plus fishing cases after the defendants had pleaded guilty.

I said, "The least you could do was make them buy a fishing license before you dismissed the charge, and the game department would at least get $7 for the cost of the license to pay for the fish they catch."

The judge thought that was a very good idea. The judge said he would do that in the future. I saw the longshoreman fishing again, and he said they had to pay through the nose for their attorney. He said he was sorry he jumped on me, and he was always friendly after that.

I learned early in my career that a person gets more with a little sugar than he does with vinegar. I always got along well with the court clerks, so I went into the clerks' office and told them whenever I had a contested case and that judge was on the bench that those were my scheduled days off. I told the clerks to set my cases before another judge, and they did. I bought them a box or two of candy for their efforts.

I didn't lose any more cases in that court. I had a good arrest record and only lost 3 cases out of 465 while working in Ohio. I lost about twenty-five cases in the first six months working in Seattle. At least we had a prosecutor to help with our cases in court. Most, however, were young and only out of law school about three months. They would all say, "I hope you brought your game code because I don't know anything about wildlife."

During the spring, wild birds and animals would start to become a nuisance. I would contact the Seattle newspaper and make a news release advising people not to pick up baby wildlife and that it was illegal to hold wildlife in captivity. The office would receive calls, and I would have to pick up baby raccoons and fawns. I also had to pick up hawks, an eagle, a young mountain lion, a wolf, and a bear cub. Some wouldn't fit into my carrying cage, so I just put them loose into the trunk of the car and closed the lid and worried about how I would get them out later.

I would turn some of them loose into the wild; others I would take to the zoo. I received a report of a person having a fawn in his backyard. I contacted the person and found a two-month-old blacktail deer fawn in a fenced backyard. He said he found it alone in the woods, so he took it home and bottle-fed it. I seized the fawn and issued him a citation for holding wildlife in captivity. He forfeited $50 bail.

One June morning, an auto repair shop called me about finding a stinking deer tail in the trunk of a wrecked car. I contacted the shop and found a blacktail deer tail behind the spare tire. I contacted the owner of the vehicle and questioned him about the deer tail. The suspect said he shot that deer over in Eastern Washington last hunting season.

I told the suspect he had a problem as the tail was not that old and there were only mule deer over in that part of the state. He finally confessed to killing it during the spring bear season in the Olympic National Forest. He was cited for killing a deer during the closed season, and he forfeited $350 bail.

The Kitsap County wildlife agent, Armon, worked out of our region office but had to cross Puget Sound on the ferry to Seattle to attend meetings. We could talk to each other on the car radio, and he asked me to come over and work deer spotlighters with him. We would pick a spot where deer frequented and wait until a car came by and then follow them to see if they were spotlighters.

In the old days, the old wardens would take the red reflectors off a stop sign and put those about four inches apart on a board and hang them in a small tree. When the poacher would shine his light on them in the field, they would glow like deer eyes. The poachers were stopped before they got too close to the reflector to know the difference. In this day and age, full-mounted decoys with turning heads are used. Too bad I didn't think of that. I had to look for a field with deer in it for bait.

Sometimes I would drive, and other times Armon would drive. He would scare the heck out of me when he drove fast without headlights following a car. I would tell him to slow down as the car was going too fast to be a spotlighter and I couldn't see the road. I told Armon I knew that if I couldn't see the road, he couldn't see it either. We never had any wrecks but did catch several spotlighting poachers.

One very dark night, I was driving and following a truck. The truck would get out of sight, and I would turn on my running light to light up the road so we wouldn't run into the ditch. The dome light in most cars was behind the driver and wouldn't provide enough light to write or read by, so I had a small white light mounted above my mirror so I could see to write tickets in the car after dark.

While following the truck for two miles and turning my running light on and off several times, I accidently turned on the white light by the mirror. Our eyes were accustomed to the dark, and Armon screamed, "Turn that damn light off! Are you trying to blind me?"

The truck stopped on a curve in front of us, and the passenger stuck the upper part of his body out of the window and pointed a rifle over the hood of the truck. After a short time, they drove on and stopped again, and then both men got out. We stopped and listened in the dark. They were making a lot of noise as if throwing trash out of the back of the truck. I turned on my red light and pulled up behind them.

Armon contacted the driver, and I contacted the passenger. A loaded .22 rimfire rifle was lying on the seat inside the truck. I didn't see any deer, but I asked the passenger, "Why didn't you shoot that deer?" The passenger said two does had crossed the road in front of them and were moving around and wouldn't hold still for him to shoot. I told Armon we had two spotlighters.

Both were arrested for hunting deer with an artificial light during the closed season, and the passenger was also cited for a LGMV. They forfeited $350 and $375 in court. We caught three more spotlighters another night. Armon wanted me to come over and work with him more often.

We had an emphasis patrol in Kitsap County with the airplane and six other cars located at different clear-cuts. Armon would ride in the plane with the pilot and give directions to us about poachers. We never found any that night and had agreed to quit the patrol at 2:00 am as the plane would be getting low on gas.

About 2:30 am, I pulled out of my spot and was heading back to the patrol cabin when Armon, in the plane said, "Bud, there is a car on the road in front of you head lighting a field."

I replied, "That is me."

Armon said, "No it's not," as I was turning a corner in the road.

Armon said, "The car just turned the corner, get on him."

I again said on the car radio, "That's me."

He replied, "No it's not."

I could hear the plane above me, so I told the officer riding with me to shine a light out the side window. Armon said, "He's spotlighting right now. Get on him." I pulled into a field and shut off my car headlights and backed up and took off down the road toward the patrol cabin. Armon said, "I'm right above him, get on him." I never answered him.

I was driving with my lights off and saw a car with its lights off coming down the road in my direction. I pulled off the road at a wide spot and waited. It was my supervisor. He said on his radio, "Looks like somebody is playing games," and we headed for the patrol cabin. Armon came in about 3:00 am and was mad at me for making him fly around in circles for a while. I told him, "I said that car was me twice, and you wouldn't believe me. So don't be mad at me." He got over it.

Once Armon drove over to King County to work spotlighters with me down by Mount Rainier. He was driving, and we parked in a wide spot at about 10:00 pm. He got out a deck of cards and wanted to play crib.

Armon also had a small white light up by his mirror, but he painted it red so it would be easier on the eyes at night. Armon turned it on so we could see to play cards. I told him, "We came here to work. I am not playing cards. Turn that light out, or the poachers will see us."

We rolled down our windows so we could listen for shots or vehicles driving on the gravel road. Several others agents were working on different road systems. The agent living in that patrol district called us on his car radio and advised that a vehicle was spotlighting on a road between his and our location. We headed that way and soon found a car with a light shining out the passenger-side window.

Armon stopped the car with his red light, and I contacted the passenger with the spotlight. There were two men in the front seat of the car and two women in the back seat. A loaded .22 rimfire rifle was on the seat between the passenger and the driver. I got the passenger out of the car and unloaded the rifle and secured it for evidence.

I put the passenger that was shining the light in the front seat of Armon's car and was questioning him about spotlighting while Armon was watching the other man and the women. The spotlighter said they had come out from Seattle to look for a deer to shoot. I was writing him a citation for spotlighting deer during the closed season, and he kept staring at the red light above Armon's mirror.

The red paint on the light had been scratched and nicked over the years, and it kinda looked like city lights in the distance on a dark night. The poacher looked at the light and asked, "Is that radar? Is that Enumclaw [the small city down in the valley]?"

I replied, "Yeah, we saw you driving up here. That's how we found you." It was nice to catch a dummy once in a while. The driver was cited for the same violation and possession of a LGMV. They later forfeited $350 and $375 in court.

A young man called me one afternoon and reported his friend for killing a deer during the closed season in another county. I took the information and contacted his friend, the violator. The suspect confessed to killing a deer up by the town of Concrete in Skagit County, but he only had half of the deer. I asked him where the rest of the deer was, and he provided me with the name and address of another suspect.

By the time I was able to contact the wildlife agent living at Concrete that night, it was 9:00 pm. We contacted the judge, who was coaching the local football game, during halftime in the locker room and obtained a search warrant for the other half of the deer at the second suspect's house. That was another first.

We arrived at the suspect's house at 10:00 pm and identified ourselves and announced that we had a warrant to search for the deer. Three hippies, two men and a woman, lived there and had the fresh-cut half deer carcass hanging on a big spike nail in the bedroom above the bed. The suspect forfeited $350 for illegal possession of deer during the closed season.

Sometimes, the information didn't always lead to an arrest. A woman in Seattle called about 10:00 pm one night and reported that her husband was hunting deer during the closed season over in Eastern Washington and would be home sometime after midnight. She wanted to remain anonymous and didn't want her husband to know she called. I told her I wouldn't tell him. I parked down the street from her house at around 11:00 pm and waited for her husband to return home.

About 5:00 am, just before daylight, the suspect arrived home with a car full of camping gear. I contacted him and advised him I was investigating a complaint about his illegal hunting. The suspect said, "That SOB, my wife called you." I asked him what made him think that. He said he and his buddies had been out drinking and his wife called and wanted him to come home. He told her he was hunting deer just so they could drink some more. I looked in his car and couldn't find any blood, hair, deer, or rifle. I told him he better use another excuse if he was going to be out all night drinking. I was tired and went home to bed.

A dead sea lion washed up on the beach near the Edmonds ferry dock and smelled pretty bad. Someone called the office and wanted it removed. The wildlife management division of the game department had a wildlife control agent position. The officer worked out of the region office and was responsible for beaver, deer, and elk damage and wildlife complaints. They also had arrest authority and would work with the wildlife agents on check stations or night patrol.

Bob Overly was the wildlife control agent for King County and worked with me a lot. Bob and I took my boat out into Puget Sound, and we met my supervisor at the beach near the ferry dock. The dead seal was about ten feet long and weighed over eight hundred pounds. We couldn't push it back into the water, so we had to wait until the tide came in more for it to float.

I tied a long rope on to it and, after a few attempts, pulled it off the beach with my boat and towed it back into Puget Sound. My supervisor told us to sink it if we could. I had an eight-foot square piece of netting with me to put over the carcass and some large rocks to tie on to the corners of the net, hoping it would sink. We waited a short time, but it wouldn't sink.

Not being familiar with marine mammals, I thought if I let the air out of the bloated carcass, it would sink. I intended on shooting a few holes into it with a single-barrel shotgun. I shot it a few times and waited, but it wouldn't go down; so I emptied the rest of the box of twenty-five shells into it. I finally realized that the blubber was not going to let it sink, no matter how many holes I put in it. We towed the smelly carcass a little farther out into the sound so it would be caught in the current of the outgoing tide and wash up on a beach in someone else's district. We never saw or heard about it again. Always have a plan.

A wildlife agent on the other side of Hood Canal called and said he received a report of shots fired during the night and that he had gone out and found deer hair and a pool of blood in the road at that location. The reporting party had obtained a car license number, which was registered to a man living in north Seattle.

A US Fish and Wildlife agent, Frank Simms, went with me to the address of the suspect and found it was a small grocery store. We went into the store in plain clothes, thinking maybe the suspect was selling the deer meat in the store.

There wasn't any meat in the store, just vegetables and boxes of health food products. I identified myself to the store owner and asked about the car. The store owner said he bought the store a year ago and didn't know where the previous owner lived. I told Frank, "Let's drive around a few blocks close to the store and see if the previous owner lives nearby. His car might be sitting on the street in front of his house." It was a real long shot!

I had only driven around two blocks when I spotted the suspect's car. Frank couldn't believe my luck. We parked behind the car, and I spotted fresh blood all over the rear bumper as we walked up to the house. I knocked on the front door, and no one came to the door. So we walked around to the backyard, and a fifty-year-old man sitting in the shade next to his garden said hello.

I identified myself and asked to speak to him in my car, where we questioned him about the shots in the night. He admitted being over there but denied shooting until I pointed out the fresh blood on his bumper. He confessed to shooting a deer and said another man with him that night was a butcher and had the deer over at his house. He said his wife had taken off with some girlfriends and that he and his buddy went out drinking. They ended up on the other side of the canal and shot the deer.

We went into his house to get the deer's heart that was in his freezer in the basement. There were three small dogs running loose in the house, and they had pooped all over the house while he and his wife were gone. There was so much dog poop on the floor we could hardly walk to the basement without stepping in it. It was another smelly mess I had gotten myself into. I issued the suspect a citation for killing a deer during the closed season and told him I would contact his buddy and arrest him also.

I advised him not to call his buddy and warn him or I would come back and arrest him for obstructing. He didn't call, and I contacted the butcher and picked up the deer for evidence and arrested him for possession of deer during the closed season. Both men forfeited $350 bail, and I called the reporting agent and advised him of finding the car and of the poaching events. A person would have a hard time doing that today as there are so many more people and cars in Washington.

I enjoyed working around the big city as I always had a lot of different violations to work on. I could make about seventy-five fishing without a license cases a year, but I tried to make different kinds of arrests as well: fishing with two poles, fishing without a steelhead punch card, failing to punch, snagging, hunting without a license, hunting without a tag, failing to tag, violating closed season rules, and hunting after-hours, etc.

I was checking fishermen on a small stream and walked up behind four men without them seeing me. I was always proud to walk up in full uniform and catch someone poaching. One didn't have a license, and I took him back to my car to write him a citation.

He asked me, "What would you have done if I had run?"

I said, "Can you run 1,500 feet per second?"

He said, "You can't shoot a man for fishing without a license." I didn't tell him if I would have shot, and he said, "Hell, you don't have to shoot anybody. You sneak up too close for them to run."

The duck season opened, and the days were clear and warm. The hunters were not having very much success, so they would stay late and hunt after-hours. I found a car parked along the river near some flooded fields and saw four hunters standing around just before dark. I pulled in behind their car with my lights out and waited for them to come to me. It was pitch-dark, and they still had not returned to their car.

Pretty soon I could hear shots coming from the field in the direction where the four hunters were standing. I walked out into the field and couldn't see the hunters, but I could see the fire from the shotgun muzzle flash in front of me as they shot at the ducks in the dark. I walked up to the first hunter and had him unload his shotgun and took his hunting license and shotshells and told him to wait by their car.

I walked up to each of the four hunters the same way in the dark, and they all thought I was one of their buddies walking up to them. The last hunter had quit shooting, and I couldn't see him in the dark. So I hollered, "Hey."

He said, "Over here," and I contacted him too. I arrested all of them for shooting one hour after legal shooting hours. They all forfeited $50 bail.

There was about 350 acres of land in the Snoqualmie Valley along the river that the department owned, and pheasants would be released for the hunters. The hunting hours ended at 4:00 pm so that the department could release the pheasants and they could find a place to roost for the night before darkness fell. The hunters would also hunt ducks on the property along the river and the sloughs, and the best shooting was just before dark.

There were three parking areas for the hunters to park their cars, and it was pretty hard for one officer to be at the right parking area to make contact with late shooters. Another officer and I were going to work late shooters, and the wildlife manager releasing the pheasants said he would stay at the middle gate to help us. I asked the other officer which parking lot he wanted to check. He took the south lot, and I took the north lot.

The duck hunters started shooting just before dark, and I walked out into the field and contacted four of them shooting a half hour late. I took their hunting license and shotshells and told them to wait in the north lot by their vehicle while I went after more late shooters. I contacted four more hunters shooting forty-five minutes late. I took their hunting license and shotshells, and we headed back to the parking area.

The other officer arrived just as I was getting into my patrol car, and he started complaining about all the shooting and not being able to catch any of the hunters. I handed him four of the licenses and told him to start writing citations for late shooting and write me down as the assisting officer. If the hunters came into court, I would come in and testify as a witness to the violation. The hunters all forfeited $50 bail.

My second elk season, I was assigned to work in the Harbor Region again. This time I would stay in a patrol cabin up on the Wynoochee River and work with John, the local officer. The night before the season opened, it snowed about six inches and all the elk were bunched up. Opening morning, a group of hunters shot up a herd and killed two cows. The assistant chief was working with John, so I met them to help investigate the violations.

They found the two dead cows and looked for a bullet in them while I followed a third blood trail down the creek and found a wounded spike elk almost dead. It was a legal animal to shoot, but nobody followed it to claim it. It was almost dead, so I shot it in the side of the head with my .38. But it didn't die, so I cut its throat. It didn't bleed very much. I gutted the spike and laid it open to cool out on the snow so the meat wouldn't spoil. I left it in the shade and went back to my car and told John about it.

The assistant chief asked if I had an elk tag. I said yes. He said, "Well, why don't you tag it?" I told him I was supposed to be working and had never killed an elk before and wanted to hunt one with my tag. If nobody found it, I would get it before dark after work and put my tag on it so the meat wouldn't go to waste. It was gone when I got back there later that afternoon.

It snowed over a foot during the night, and we couldn't get around in our Matadors. So we went back to the office and got a four-wheel drive Blazer to drive. John received a call about another cow elk killed in a closed area and how the meat had been taken. We looked for the kill site for about an hour and couldn't find it. John and I couldn't agree on which direction to go back to the Blazer. He worked the area, so I let him pull rank.

After another hour looking for our vehicle, I saw a grouse and asked John if he thought I should shoot it for something to eat in the event we had to spend the night in the woods. I didn't shoot it and finally convinced John to go in the direction I thought he parked our ride home. We found the Blazer, then John remembered another road system that would take us to the kill site. We found the gut pile and looked for a bullet.

I had a plastic sandwich bag in my pocket and put it on my hand and went through the stomach and fecal matter feeling for a bullet. I found what appeared to be the lead core of a .270-caliber bullet. John had a list of cow permit holders and knew where a local hunter suspect was camped. We contacted the hunter and questioned him about the illegal cow kill. He was nervous but wouldn't admit killing the cow. He said he lost his elk tag and he and his buddies were in town yesterday drinking all day.

I told John, "I bet the hunter took the elk meat into town to his dad's house. Let's go into town and ask his dad to see the meat." We knocked on the door and asked the man if we could get a harvest report for the cow elk his son killed. The man said, "Sure, come on in. It's in the freezer." We seized the meat for evidence and went back and arrested the son for killing an elk in a closed area. He was found guilty in court. I was finally getting to think like an elk hunter; sometimes it pays to play a hunch.

My car was almost out of gas one afternoon when I returned home from checking fishermen all day, and I figured I would just gas up the next morning before driving too far. The state patrol radio dispatch called me around 11:00 pm and advised me a bear had been hit by a car but was not dead about five miles from my house. The gas stations were all closed on my way there, but I figured I had enough gas to reach another station before I took the bear to hang in the cooler at the fish hatchery.

When I arrived at the scene, I was distracted by all the people standing around the injured bear, and I got out and left my car motor running. A deputy sheriff was there directing traffic and two hippies, a man and woman, had a small rope tied to the bear's neck and was kneeling beside it, petting it. I told them to get away from the 125 pound injured bear as it was dangerous.

The bear had blood coming out of its mouth, and I knew it had broken ribs and internal damage and wouldn't live very long. I asked the deputy if he had a shotgun in his patrol car to use to shoot the bear and put it out of its misery. The hippies didn't want me to shoot it. I told them to stand back; it was the humane thing to do. The deputy went to get his shotgun, and I reached down and took the rope off the bear's neck and asked the hippie if he wanted his rope.

The injured bear got up and fell down then got up again. I was following it, trying to put the rope back on its neck. The bear went through a wooden board fence by the road into a horse pasture with me still following it, trying to put the rope back onto it. Why, I don't know? The injured bear backed up to a small pine tree and growled at me. I said to myself, "What are you doing?" I had sold my old .38 special and bought a new model 66 Smith & Wesson .357 Mag with a holster, and I sewed ammo loops on the gun belt to hold six extra cartridges.

I pulled out my .357 Mag pistol and shot it in the head, killing it. I pulled the bear back through the fence to my car and found my car had run out of gas. The state troopers had a small pump in their car trunk to pump a gallon of gas into the car of stranded motorists on the freeway. The deputy didn't have that capability, so I had to call radio dispatch and ask if a trooper could come and give me a gas assist. I was pretty embarrassed.

The gallon of gas was enough for me to get to another gas station and fill up my tank. A lesson learned: always have enough gas to go out again at night on a complaint. I put the bear on the trunk of my car and took it to the fish hatchery and skinned it. I put the carcass in the cooler and called a charitable organization, and they processed the meat for human consumption.

Some people couldn't eat beef and would get a letter from their doctor to eat wild game meat. Wildlife officers would donate road kill and confiscated fish and game meat, if it was fit to eat, to this list of people for consumption and obtain a receipt of the transaction for their records or for court evidence.

The Seattle area had a lot of waterfowl living and staying on Lake Washington and all the other small lakes in the city year-round because there wasn't any hunting pressure to disperse them. Our region office would receive a lot of complaints about ducks and geese messing up swimming pools and pooping on the lawns of homeowners and golf course putting greens. The office would refer the complaints to the US Fish and Wildlife Service since they managed migratory waterfowl.

US Fish and Wildlife agent Richard Lichtenberg asked me to help investigate a complaint of a man trapping ducks in Downtown Seattle on Lake Union. We sat in an empty apartment across the street from the suspect's house and waited to see what transpired. About 10:00 pm, a man came out of the suspect's house with a bucket and walked down to the edge of the lake. He threw some corn on the ground, and the mallard ducks came out of the water and ate it.

The man waited until the ducks ate all the corn, and then he dropped a little more on the ground as he walked back to the house. The ducks would eat the corn and follow the man back across the street to the house. The man opened the door of the house and walked in and threw some corn on the floor. About twenty-five ducks walked into the house, and then the man shut the door behind them.

Richard and I went and knocked on the door of the house and contacted the suspect. The suspect opened the door and let us in. The suspect had newspaper spread all over the floor to make it easier to clean up the duck poop. The suspect said he was just feeding the ducks. After they ate the corn, he would let them out and the ducks would go back to the lake.

He said he fed them every night. We checked his trash can and freezer and couldn't find any blood, feathers, duck meat, or cages to put the ducks into for transportation. The suspect was given a verbal warning for holding waterfowl in captivity and advised to just feed the ducks outside by the lake in the future. It takes all kind of people to make the world go 'round.

In 1973, the state patrol invited the wildlife agents to shoot in a combat pistol match with their troopers. I was probably at the height of my shooting ability and won the match several times, so they put me in a distinguished master class. But I still won! They finally quit asking us to participate. I didn't have any buddy who wanted to shoot in competition matches with me, so I soon lost interest in pistol shooting. But I did try to beat the other wildlife agents when we had to qualify.

The wildlife agents carried all different kinds of sidearms, and we looked unprofessional when we were gathered together. I told the chief that the department should provide qualification training and maintain records to prevent a big lawsuit against the department and an officer in the event a shooting incident occurred. Better yet, the department should provide sidearms so everyone looked the same and more professional.

In September of 1974, three other officers and I were sent to an NRA Firearms Instructor Training School to be certified instructors for the department. The department purchased a stainless model 66 Smith & Wesson .357 Mag revolver, belt, holster, and drop-down ammo pouches for each officer. When the revolvers arrived, we hand-inspected the revolvers, dry-fired them, wrote down the serial numbers, and assigned them to the rest of the officers.

One of the instructors wanted to pick out the best revolver for himself and had a half dozen lying all around him and couldn't make up his mind on which one he wanted. I was dry-firing one with nice grips, with a smooth action, and said, "I'll take this one." The next week, when we test-fired all of them, mine shot the tightest group. We started qualifying twice a year, and the division maintained the records in Olympia.

I was patrolling the national forest near Stampede Pass north of Mount Rainier the day before elk season opened. Radio dispatch called for any officer working east of Mount Rainier. I answered and said I was about ten miles away. A deer hunter had observed two men killing a bull elk and was standing by the poachers' vehicle. Another officer, Terry Hoffer, who worked that area heard the radio traffic and advised that he was en route and for me to try to get there from my location. I told Terry I would try.

Still driving my two-wheel drive Matador, I had to cross over a mountain ridge on a jeep-rutted, two-track logging skid road to get there. I could just squeeze my car between two five-feet-in-diameter stumps and, with the pedal to the metal, was able to get there without getting stuck. I advised the other officer that I had made it and was going to be out of my car contacting the reporting party. I contacted the reporting party and took down the poachers' descriptions and kill site information and thanked the reporting party.

The reporting party was going to go back to the kill site to see if the poachers were still there while I waited at the vehicle. I moved my car down the road, out of sight of the poachers' truck, and put on a red hat and my favorite red-and-green plaid wool shirt over my uniform and stood near the trail. An hour later a man, matching the description of one of the poachers, came walking down the trail to his truck.

The reporting party was walking a short distance behind him on the trail and nodded that he was one of the poachers. I let the suspect approach to within four feet of me and said, "State wildlife agent," and showed him my badge on my uniform shirt. I asked to see his hunting license and took his rifle.

He still had a little fresh blood on his pant legs and I advised him that he was under arrest for killing an elk during the closed season. Terry and another officer arrived in another car just as I reached the poacher's truck. I turned the poacher over to Terry to question and to take to jail. The reporting party helped pack out the elk meat for evidence. The second officer, Jeff Boone, and I drove a lower road system looking for the poacher's son.

A small pickup truck with two male hunters approached us, and we stopped to talk to them. Upon checking their license, we found the driver (I will call him Bob) to be the poacher's son and fitting the description of the second poacher at the kill site. The passenger (I will call him Jim) had fresh blood under his fingernails. I asked Jim if he had killed a deer, and he stated no. He had already killed his deer last week. Jim had a fresh deer heart in his day pack, so I asked Jim to step over to my car and questioned him away from Bob.

Jim said the heart belonged to the deer that Bob had just killed. Jim said he gutted the deer for Bob and that was why he had blood on his hands. The deer season was open, so I questioned Bob in his truck. He still had an unnotched deer tag with his hunting license. He said he wasn't going to say anything about who killed the deer. It was getting too dark to hike back up the mountain to see if he could find the deer.

I held the deer heart for evidence of Jim killing two deer in one year and advised him that I would do a little more investigating before he was charged with killing two deer. I would contact him at his home later. In hindsight, I should have gone there that night. I told Bob he was going to be charged with aiding in the killing of an elk during the closed season.

I told Bob I didn't believe he killed any deer today and to meet me back there alone at daylight and we would go and see if he could find the dead deer tomorrow. If he couldn't find it, Jim would also be charged with wastage of a big game animal. At daylight the next morning, Terry Hoffer and I arrived and waited for Bob to show up. Bob showed up with Jim, the same passenger as yesterday.

I told Jim he was not going up the hill to look for the deer. We got into a heated argument, and he said, "You can't keep me from walking in the woods on forest service land." I told Jim maybe not, but if he gave any kind of directions, I could arrest him for interfering with my investigation. If he didn't get out of my face, I would arrest him for obstructing.

Terry and I must have been tired from working too many hours as we just looked at each other and let Jim accompany us up the mountain. I wanted to go with the other officer to help drag the evidence deer back to the car. I told Bob to walk in the front and find the deer. Terry and I walked between Bob and Jim, and I told Jim not to point or give any assistance to his friend.

About halfway to the deer, Jim started saying we were drifting too far to the left. I told him not to give any more directions or he would be arrested. We got into a real heated argument again and stood nose to nose for a few minutes before he backed down. Jim worked as a logger in the woods and was bigger than Terry and me. We would have had our hands full if he started swinging and they both jumped on us.

I saw some camp robbers (gray jays) as we were getting close to the top of the hill and knew the deer was not too far off to our left. Bob didn't know where the deer was and was drifting over to the right again. Jim yelled, "Here it is," and ran over to the deer carcass. The deer was not tagged, and I told Bob he hadn't killed the deer and wouldn't have found it without his friend. I would hold the deer for evidence and contact the prosecutor to see what charges would be filed.

A new inexperienced prosecutor charged Bob with aiding and abetting in the killing of an elk during the closed season. He charged Jim with killing two deer in one year and then dismissed the aiding charge on Bob to have him testify that Jim killed the deer. The prosecutor shouldn't have dismissed the aiding charge until after the deer case was heard in court. Bob came into court and changed his story and said he shot the deer, and the case against Jim was dismissed.

I didn't like the outcome, but some things I had no control of. Trying to be a Monday morning quarterback wasn't going to help either. Looking back on the case, I should have arrested Jim for obstructing and took him to jail. We could have come back later with Bob to look for the deer or Terry could have gone alone with Bob to look for the deer carcass.

Without handcuffs or a cage in my car, it would have been a real dogfight to get Jim to jail or even to keep him there for two hours until a deputy could get there to transport him. I had his name and address. I could also have let him go and arrest him another day; however, he wouldn't leave when told to go back to the truck. I will never know. On a sad note, Terry was killed checking elk hunters in 1984 when a hunter tried to unload a rifle inside a jeep. The rifle discharged, and the bullet went through the side of the jeep and through Terry's truck door and struck Terry in the chest, killing him. It was a very sad event.

Tribal hunters were shooting cow elk down by Mount Rainier during the elk season, so another officer and I were assigned to work a plainclothes patrol in an unmarked vehicle. About 10:00 am, we pulled into a wooded area and parked near several hunter vehicles. Just as we got out of our jeep, we heard a rifle shot about three hundred yards away in the woods. I waited by the vehicles while my buddy went into the timber to look around.

I was wearing a red hat, my favorite red-and-green plaid wool shirt, and green wool pants and had a rifle leaning up against an old red jeep. I was standing around as if waiting for my hunting buddy to return to the jeep. After about a half hour, a hunter came out of the woods carrying a five-point bull elk head. I couldn't see any tag attached to the antlers and was going to identify myself after he set the head down.

The hunter asked, "What day is it?" It was the first day of the elk season, and I knew what day it was. But I said, "I think it is the fifth." The hunter said, "I couldn't remember what day it was and haven't notched my tag yet," and took out his elk tag and started to notch the day and month. He said, "You're the game warden, aren't you?" I asked him what gave him that idea. He said he saw me once in a restaurant in Bothell, the town forty-five miles away where I lived.

I told him he better learn to start notching his tag at the kill site before he got back to his vehicle. If a hunter was back at his vehicle with an unnotched tag, he was issued a ticket because it was so easy to take the untagged animal home and come back another day and hunt on the same tag. He was given a verbal warning. I couldn't believe I had such a handsome face and lots of people knew me!

I was working the pheasant release area in the Snoqualmie Valley and trying to keep some sense of order among the hunters. They would keep asking, "Is it eight o'clock yet?" and keep edging closer to the hunting area. I would tell them, "You have ten minutes yet. Set your watches." I left to go to the other parking lot and went through the same scenario with them.

At eight o'clock, a whistle would blow in town to signal the start of the workday for one of the local businesses. I would say, "Okay," and the hunters would run as fast as they could out into the fields, racing the other hunters. Running with a loaded shotgun wearing hip boots in mud was very dangerous.

One of the hunters had a black lab retriever that would take off and not respond to his commands. The hunter would scream at the top of his lungs, "Bobby, Bobby, damn you, come back here." The dog would be running ahead of the hunters, flushing all the pheasants before they were close enough for a shot. The hunter was very rude to other hunters, so I went out into the field and contacted him.

I saw him shoot a pheasant, and he turned and saw me and just left the pheasant lying on the ground and kept yelling for his dog. I checked his license and noticed a large lump in the back of his coat and asked to check the pheasants in his coat. He pulled out two dead rooster pheasants, and I told him, "With that dead one on the ground in front of you, that makes you over your limit."

I put the three pheasants in a pile and knelt down to write the hunter a citation. The hunter kept yelling at his dog and waving the shotgun around in a dangerous manner. He just went ballistic and started cursing and yelling louder. I was in a real bad position to defend myself and could feel the hair stand up on the back of my neck again. I stood up and again told him to unload his shotgun. He was swinging the shotgun all around and still wouldn't unload it.

My sidearm was under my raincoat and I had no way to get to it. I felt I was very close to getting shot. Most uniform coats and rain gear at that time didn't have a slot or area left open to make a sidearm available to the officer. I don't wear a sidearm to try a quick draw but wear it to defend myself in the event someone is threatening my life or another officer.

The hunter's buddy came up and was standing next to us. I told him to tell the suspect to calm down before things got worse. The hunter still refused to unload his shotgun or quit yelling. It had started raining harder, so I told the hunter, "I can't write this ticket out here in the rain. Let's go to my car by the road," and in the same motion, I reached over and took the shotgun from the hunter and unloaded it.

We all walked to my car, and I issued a citation for killing over the limit of pheasants, with a $50 bail. The hunter forfeited bail and never came to court to face the judge. The hunter kept hunting on the release site but did get a different dog that didn't respond any better than the first one. I am beginning to see why the previous officer had problems with violators. They have bad attitudes. Size doesn't seem to matter to them.

In 1974, a Ninth Circuit federal court judge raised up his ugly head and spit on all the fishermen in the state of Washington when he issued the now famous Boldt decision. Indian tribes in Washington had sued the state, claiming they had a right to net steelhead.

After many years of court battles, the Ninth Circuit reversed an earlier court case and said the tribes had a right to half of the fish in the state in their ceded treaty area and also gave them half of the hatchery fish the state raised with money from sport license dollars. All the fishermen were mad as hell.

Every time I checked a steelhead fisherman in the winter, I would have to explain the Boldt decision to them. The fishermen would be standing elbow to elbow, six feet apart on the banks of the rivers. As I explained the decision to one fisherman, the other one heard it too, but I would have to explain it all over again, again and again. The fishermen were mad at me and the game department.

I told them to be mad at the court that issued the decision, not at me or the department. It was hard trying to be nice to the fishermen. It would drain all the energy out of me by the end of the day, and I was beginning to hate checking steelheaders. I would have nightmares about checking steelhead fishermen.

The tribes started setting steelhead netting seasons, and they took a lot of fish out of the river system. The tribes also wanted fish for subsistence and ceremony events, thereby taking way over their 50 percent. The sport fishermen started catching fewer and fewer fish and got madder and madder at me and the department. The tribes wouldn't and didn't obey the tribal fishing seasons, and the sport fishermen got even madder. The Indians said, "We fish on Indian time, not white man's time."

The game department started instructing the wildlife agents to pull the illegal nets and turn them over to the tribal enforcement officers. Larry would bring his fourteen-foot boat, and we would pull nets out of the ship canal and Lake Washington at all hours of the night on weekends and holidays. We would have the small boat piled high with the three-hundred-foot gill nets. The tribe would only fine the tribal violators $25 for catching hundreds of dollars' worth of fish. At least it took the illegal fishermen a week turnaround time to get their nets back, and they lost hundreds of dollars by not being able to fish.

I received a new patrol vehicle, another car that didn't have air-conditioning or four-wheel drive. Cars work great driving in town and to meetings but are unable to drive in the mountains in ten inches of snow to check hunters. I had to jack up the suspension so it wouldn't drag on the country roads.

A new patrol vehicle

One evening, I was waiting at the boat launch for Larry to come help me pull another illegal net out of Lake Washington. A truck with three half-drunk male Indians drove up to me parked under the bridge. The Indians got out and started arguing with me. They wanted to know what I was doing there. I was standing outside my car, and the three subjects circled around me and started to get more aggressive. It was dark under the bridge, and nobody could see us. It was a bad place to get into a fight.

I had been trained in the use of the baton when I worked in Ohio. I had my heavy five-cell flashlight in my left hand, and I raised it up to my shoulder, as if trying to shine it on them to see. From that position, it would be very easy to use it and defend myself. It seemed to deter the three subjects, and they got back into their truck and drove away. I drove over to an old pier where I could see the net in the lake in case the three subjects took their boat and started pulling it.

Larry came with his boat, and we pulled the illegal net. After we loaded his boat on his trailer, he took me back to my car. As we pulled into the parking lot by the pier, I could see a lot of paper on the ground. I said to Larry, "Someone had a lot of nerve dumping that litter right beside my car." As we got closer, I said, "Hell, that is my stuff out of my car." Someone had broken into it while we were pulling the net.

The thief took my jockey box containing fishing and hunting pamphlets, my ticket book, notebooks, and loose papers and threw it on the ground beside my car. I had a rifle scabbard tied to the front of the front seat of my car. It held a three-foot riot stick and a .30-30 Winchester rifle that I used to shoot crippled animals. The thief stole my am radio from under the dashboard, several knives I had in the box, and the riot stick but missed the rifle. I never found out who did it. I guess it could have been worse.

An anonymous caller called the region office to report that a large amount of steelhead was being stored in a commercial fish warehouse on the waterfront. Larry and I contacted the foreman at the Rainier Cold Storage Facility and asked to inspect their fish ticket records. Fish buyers were required to fill out a fish ticket for each purchase of steelhead or salmon from a fisherman to monitor the harvest on a river system.

We found that a fish buyer had brought in eighteen thousand pounds of steelhead from the Columbia River to have frozen for resale. In my limited experience working in the Northwest, I had only seen steelhead in the wild or fresh caught on the riverbank. After the steelhead were flash frozen, I couldn't tell them from salmon. The fish buyer didn't document where the steelhead came from, so Larry said, "Seize the fish until we can find out where they came from." We took three one-hundred-pound boxes of three different weight sizes and held them for evidence.

The foreman was advised that the rest of the steelhead from that fish buyer was to be seized and he was not to release them to anyone. I was worried I would be sued as the eighteen thousand pounds of fish was worth a little more than the spare change I had lying around the house. Larry said, "Ahh, don't worry."

Now I had to find a place to store the evidence. We rented a locker in another frozen food market and put a lock on the unit to keep it secure until the investigation was complete. The fish buyer was charged in court for failing to document the steelhead catch area. Without accurate fish harvest numbers, the tribes would keep netting and exceed their 50 percent. The fish buyer hired a lawyer and was only fined $100 and got the fish back. Heck of a deal for him.

The federal government passed the Marine Mammal Act, and our department was given some money for enforcement. The department bought a new nineteen-foot Glasply inboard boat to use to patrol Puget Sound for violations. It would go about forty knots on the flat water but wasn't quite big enough for rough water and high winds. It was assigned to me and parked on a trailer at the office.

Since the biggest boat I had ever operated was a fourteen-foot outboard, I took a class in 1975 on basic seamanship and boat handling put on by the coast guard auxiliary. The course was ten weeks' long, four hours a night, one night a week. It was very interesting, and I learned about all the different lights and buoys along the rivers and ocean. We were tested on how to read charts and navigate by compass and boat safety.

Years ago, my grampa once told me, "All work and no play makes Jack a dull boy." The department had a pretty relaxed policy of use of state equipment and promoted family bonding, as one would say. I took my son with me a lot of times in the state car when I had to pick up orphan wildlife, on wildlife counts or to make fish plants in beaver ponds.

Sometimes, if the officers had a license, he would shoot a deer or elk during the season while he was on patrol. I guess that was a fringe benefit for being called out to arrest a violator or pick up road kills at midnight on a day off.

The long day patrolling on Puget Sound in the boat would take us away from all the fast-food restaurants in town, so we would pack a sack lunch. Sometimes we would drop a hook and line over the side of the boat while we ate our lunch. We were amazed at the number of rockfish, true cod, lingcod, and halibut that laid in the bottom of the boat after lunch!

Friends came over for my thirty-fifth birthday, and we were sitting around the table talking about getting older. A lady friend asked me if I felt any older. I replied, "I don't think so. I can still run just as fast as I ever did." She said, "Yeah, but can you run as far?" I replied, "I don't know. I never tried to see how far I could run."

The very next night I was checking for hunters shooting after legal shooting hours in the valley. I found a car parked by a small lake and could see four duck hunters standing around just before dark, so I waited for them to return to the car. Twenty five minutes after dark, I heard shooting coming from their direction, and I headed out into the field toward the lake. I met the duck hunters at the edge of the lake. They denied shooting after-hours and said some other hunters did the shooting. I asked to see their hunting license, and the other group of hunters started shooting again. I held their license and told them to wait by my car until I returned. I went around the lake and heard more shooting and saw fire come out of four gun barrels in the dark ahead of me.

I approached in the dark, and when I was standing next to the first hunter, I turned on my flashlight. The four hunters took off running to the south, away from my car. I had hip boots on as I ran after them but was able to stay about twenty-five yards behind them. I told them to stop, but they crossed a fence and headed toward a house sitting farther off the road. The same house where Larry and I took the illegal deer out of the barn's rafters.

I saw the hunters drop a couple ducks near the fence. If I shined my light on them to keep track of them, they could see where they were running, so I turned my light off. There was a pole light near the barn. It lighted up the area in front of the hunters, and I could see them as they ran in front of me.

They ran around the back of the house, so I ran toward the front door. Just as I walked past the big picture window, I saw the hunters coming into the house through the back door. I knocked on the front door, and a lady opened it. I was so out of breath from running five hundred yards I could hardly talk to her. I was in uniform and told her I chased four duck hunters into her house and wanted to talk to them.

She said, "Come on in. I don't even know those guys." I stepped into the front room and found one of the hunters lying on the floor behind the couch. I asked him where his buddies were, and the son of the lady came out of the bedroom—the same person I had arrested for the illegal deer several years earlier.

I asked the first hunter again, "Where are your buddies?" and two more of them came out of the bedroom. The lady's son had on clean dry clothes, but the three duck hunters had on wet muddy clothes. I asked again where the fourth hunter was. They said he stayed outside with the shotguns. I took identification from the three suspects and looked out the back of the house with my flashlight but couldn't find him.

Advising the three they were under arrest for shooting afterhours, I returned to my car to get court information for them. They were advised not to leave. I went back to pick up the two ducks by the fence and went to my car. I gave the first four hunters waiting by their car back their licenses and thanked them for their patience and explained catching the other four.

I called Larry on the radio, and he arrived just as I returned to the house. We were unable to locate the fourth hunter or the shotguns. Thinking like a Monday morning quarterback, I should have told the three they were going to spend a night in jail unless the fourth hunter came forward. Larry and I must have been working too many hours and didn't want to have to work another two hours and take them all to jail. I just issued the three on hand citations for hunting after-hours.

The next day I recontacted the hunter that I found behind the couch and questioned him about his fourth buddy. He said I didn't catch him hunting and they were going to get an attorney and beat the tickets in court. Besides, I couldn't run fast enough to catch him. I replied, "Well, I ran fast enough to see you coming in the back door." He wouldn't give up his buddy, and the three never came to court and forfeited $50 bail. It's was hard for me to think about all my options when I was out of breath. At least I learned how far I could run.

The either-sex deer season opened up in the river bottom to remove some deer that were causing a lot of vehicle accidents and damage to gardens and flowers beds. It had rained during the night, and I was patrolling a closed area and saw fresh vehicle tracks in the gravel road. I followed the tracks about five miles to a station wagon parked by a clear-cut. I walked over to three people standing by the edge of a steep drop-off.

Two young ladies and a man were looking down at something in the clear-cut. I walked over to them in full uniform and could see two men dragging two dead bucks up the hill toward them. I said, "I see they killed a couple bucks." The closest lady said yes.

One of the hunters looked up at me and asked "Who is that?"

The lady looked at the Red Cross patch on my right shoulder and asked, "Who are you?"

I said, "The game warden."

She yelled back down the hill, "The game warden." I had not said anything about the season being closed, but the hunter said, "Oh, ahh, we didn't know the season was closed here."

I said, "Well, come up here and let me get some information from you." It was kinda funny, me talking to the lady and her talking to the hunter. I called Larry and asked him to help me retrieve the dead deer for evidence. The hill was too steep for one man to drag a deer up by himself.

Larry and I tied four pieces of rope together and tied it to his truck and to one of the bucks. The antlers would get caught in the brush when he drove forward, so I had to go down the hill and hold on to the rope and hold the deer's head up as he pulled forward with his truck. I should have tied it by the back legs.

Larry could only drive about twenty-five yards and have to back up and retie the rope and pull forward again. The rope broke twice, and it took us over an hour to get both deer up the hill. I issued a citation to both hunters for hunting deer in a closed area, and they both forfeited $350 in court.

I was sitting in the office one morning reading the local newspaper about someone stealing fur pelts from a fur buyer in Oregon. The secretary came back and said, "That's funny. Three young guys just came in and bought trapping license. The season closes tomorrow." I looked at the license stubs at the front desk and wrote down the name and addresses of the three subjects. I contacted the Goldberg fur buyer business in Seattle the next day and spoke with the owner about the fur theft report in the newspaper.

He was the biggest fur buyer in the Northwest and had employees working out of vans buying fur in small towns in other states. One of his employees spent the night in a motel near Portland and had the van parked in the parking lot. Someone broke into it and stole all the raw fur pelts worth about $2,000.

I told him, "I may have several suspects," and asked to check his records to see if he purchased any fur pelts from the three suspects. His records showed he had purchased a list of fur pelts for $2,125 from the three just after they purchased the trapping license. I told him to hold the furs for evidence until I could contact the suspects. I contacted the suspect that lived the closest to me and questioned him about selling the fur pelts.

The suspect said he had trapped in Washington with his buddies on the Snohomish River and they had trapped those pelts from the river. There were some nutria pelts in the stolen furs, and they were not native to the Snohomish River. I could tell he was lying. I set him up with a trick question and said, "You sure took good care of those pelts. Did you use a wooden box trap or a neck trap?" He said, "A box trap."

I said, "You're lying. You have to use leg hold traps, and nutria are not native to this area. You stole those fur pelts down in Portland and bought the trapping license so you could sell them." The suspect kept denying stealing the fur pelts. I told him he was lying, but I didn't have jurisdiction in Oregon and didn't witness the violation. So I would have to contact the prosecutor and provide him with all the facts. He would be charged with theft and receive something in the mail with court information at a later date.

I contacted the other two suspects, but their buddy had already called them. They wouldn't say anything. The three suspects lived in Snohomish County, so I took the information to the Snohomish County prosecutor. He said the violation didn't occur in Snohomish County or his jurisdiction and so he wouldn't file any thief charges on the three subjects since I couldn't prove they possessed the fur pelts in Snohomish County.

I contacted the USFW office to see if they could charge the three with the Lacey Act violation of interstate transportation of wildlife parts. They said it was private property and didn't want to get involved. I sent the information to the Oregon sheriff department to see if they would prosecute. I was never called to testify, so I don't think the suspects were ever charged for the theft. It was easy money if you didn't get shot stealing.

The game department adopted new rules and regulations on sale and possession of wildlife parts. This was good news because working in the biggest city in the state, I ran into violations of just about every statute of the game code. I had a lot of pet shops, taxidermists, and fur dealers in my patrol district and would check their license and inspect the wildlife. The new rules required the taxidermist to keep a ledger with the name, address, and license information on all the wildlife parts in their shop.

The chief and assistant chief came up to Seattle to meet with all the taxidermists and wanted me to go along. I think they just wanted a driver and didn't want to have to find a place to park their car. They would explain the new rules and ledger, and when asked a question, they would look at me and ask, "What do you think, Bud?" I was humbled they would ask me for my opinion. They were the top brass in the enforcement division and should be the ones to dictate law and policy!

I told them what I wanted in the ledger to make it easy to find illegal wildlife parts. The new rules and regulation changes helped fill in some of the loopholes in the game code. I still felt the WGD had not caught up to the real world and was now only about twenty-five years behind modern times.

The court system issued a new bigger citation book and raised the bail amounts for wildlife violations. Misdemeanors went up to $50, and gross misdemeanors went up to $450. We were issued a bigger aluminum carrying box for the citation book that wouldn't even fit into our coat pockets and made it harder to carry them while on foot patrol on the rivers.

The department made some administrative changes and reduced the number of regions down to six and made a supervisory position for the wildlife agents. They were called area supervisory agents (ASA). A lot of the officers and I took the oral test.

I felt the "good old boy" syndrome still existed in the game department, and even before I knew what the test scores were, I guessed the names of about 80 percent of those who would be appointed supervisors. The senior most officer in the area. My good friend Larry was promoted and would be my immediate supervisor. That was okay; I liked Larry and could work for him.

I was next in line for a promotion on the Westside of the state after the first positions were filled. A few years later, an ASA passed away and a vacancy occurred. I was offered the promotion. I would have to move and relocate to Enumclaw, a small city in southern King County.

My wife and I had started an antique business to make extra money. I would refinish old furniture on my days off, and we would sell it in our garage. I was burning the candle at both ends trying to make enough money to satisfy my wife and to make enough arrests to keep the state happy. I wanted to move, but my family didn't want to. So I turned the promotion down.

After the Boldt decision, the Indian tribes were setting salmon and steelhead net seasons out in Puget Sound and causing a lot of conflict with the commercial salmon gill net fishermen. The department of fisheries patrol officers had jurisdiction of food fish, salmon, and shellfish and enforced their rules and regulations. The gill netters were also mad about the Boldt decision, and gunshots were exchanged with patrol officers.

The fisheries department would ask the wildlife agents to help patrol the sound for netting violations. The federal government gave both state agencies money to hire more officers and purchase more equipment to patrol the sound.

The game department purchased bulletproof vests, handcuffs, Mace, and new ammo pouches that held two speed loaders for all the officers. We started getting more training in defensive tactics and cuffing violators. A twenty-five-foot twin-engine patrol boat was also purchased for our region. It was stored in the marina by the locks on Puget Sound, and they wanted Larry to be in charge of operating it on Puget Sound. That left Larry's ASA position and patrol district vacant.

The department was hiring more wildlife agents and held another training school in Olympia. I was asked to teach the new cadets the rules and regulations, the game code, and search and seizure authority. I felt it was a great honor to be asked again to teach other officers what I thought our laws meant—something the chief or regional agent with a lot more years of experience should be doing.

I also assisted with the firearms training. After going over the classroom portion on firearm safety, we went out to the range. I was standing on the seven-yard line facing a man-sized silhouette target and teaching sight alignment. I pulled out my service revolver and told the cadets that if the front sight was perfectly aligned in the notch of the rear sight, they would hit the target every time.

Aligning the sights, I shot at a small one-inch square beside the head of the target and hit it. I turned the revolver on its left side and hit it again. I turned the revolver on its right side and hit it a third time. I told the cadets this was how the Polish shoot, and then I turned the revolver upside down, held the grip with my right thumb and forefinger, and used my little (pinky) finger to pull the trigger. I hit the target the fourth time. The cadets were amazed. Later that day, after they had completed firing a sixty-round qualification course, they wanted to see me shoot again.

I was standing on the sixty-yard line, ten yards farther back then they had been shooting, and the range was clear of other officers. I pulled out my revolver and turned it upside down and shot at a metal silhouette target, hitting it in the center. They said, "Let's see you do that again."

I said, "If any of you can do it in one shot, I'll do it again."

I have learned over my years of showing off and trick shooting to never do it the second time. The results may not always be the same. The cadets tried for over a half hour and couldn't hit the metal target, so I never had to shoot again.

I was heading out to do a night patrol with another officer in the Stampede Pass area when radio dispatch advised me to call the chief. In that day and age, one would wonder what he did wrong when asked to call the chief. I stopped at the Tokul Creek hatchery and called Olympia for the chief. He said, "Bud, you want a promotion?"

I was next in line on the personnel list for a promotion. I asked, "Where?"

He said, "Carnation."

I said, "I only live twenty miles from there. Can I supervise from Bothell until I can move at a later date?"

He said, "I think we can work that out," and in October of 1977, I was promoted to wildlife agent II, Larry's ASA position. It was a pretty laid-back process, but it was official.

PROMOTED TO SUPERVISOR

A new cadet filled my station, so I supervised five officers and one control agent. I also got a new patrol vehicle, a truck for pulling the nineteen-foot boat, and a portable radio. The standard one seat truck was green and just two-wheel drive and still didn't have air-conditioning. It was nice to patrol in and haul evidence with, but it made it difficult to interview suspects with another officer in the rain. Someone had to stand out in the rain!

Being a supervisor, I could schedule the other agents to cover my district while I was on vacation and was able to work in a ten day hunt for caribou and moose in Alaska. My game biologist friend from Ohio moved up there in 1976, and he and his son would hunt with me.

The deer season opened, and Bob and I were working the Spur 10 check station. About midmorning, a truck with a canopy pulled up to the intersection and stopped. I approached the driver's side and observed three Hispanic males. They were trying to hide a .22 rimfire rifle with their feet and legs.

The rifle was illegal to hunt deer with, so I asked the driver what he was hunting with the .22. He replied, "Chicken-like birds."

I asked, "Grouse?"

He said, "No, chicken-like birds."

I said, "Ducks?" He again replied no. Apparently, he didn't know the English word for whatever it was he wanted to say. I asked the driver to step out of the truck and found the rifle loaded.

I asked to see his hunting license, and he replied that he didn't have one. I asked if either of the other men had a license, and they replied no. They were working thinning trees for the Weyerhaeuser Timber Company. I could hear noise coming from the back of the pickup and asked the driver what was in the back of his truck. He replied, "Other workers." I asked Bob to come and stand by the driver while I opened the back of the truck. I opened the canopy door and saw a large group of Hispanic men lying on an old mattress.

I ask them all to step out of the truck. There were thirteen of them. There was a lump under the mattress after they got off of it. I pulled up the corner and saw a small blacktail deer fawn. I pulled the doe fawn out, and it was so little I could hold it up with one hand. I told Bob, "Look, they shot Bambi."

They had a contract with the timber company, so I figured the driver would take care of the ticket. The season was only open for buck deer, so I issued a citation for possession of a doe deer during the closed season and for possession of a LGMV. The driver posted and forfeited $500, and the rifle was confiscated by the court since he was an alien.

There is a small dam at the end of the ship canal between Lake

Union and Puget Sound with a set of locks to let commercial boat traffic through. A fish ladder was built on the other end of the dam to let salmon and steelhead go upstream into several lakes and streams to spawn. People would fish below the ladder and occasionally go up and snag a fish out of the ladder and take it downstream as a legal catch.

A group of four juveniles who were always fishing below the ladder would do most of the snagging. The lockmaster would call the office, and radio dispatch would call me. By the time I got there, they were gone. I would lie in the bushes at night trying to catch them but never did. The raccoons would be surprised and would growl at me when they prowled in the bushes at night. I was happy they never bit me.

One night a gill net was tied off the wing pier below the locks during the closed season for the Indian fishery. It was reported that it belonged to one of the juveniles who would than sell the steelhead he caught to local fishermen. Two other officers and I positioned ourselves at locations where we could observe the net and hopefully catch the suspect.

About midnight, the officer on the north side of the bay advised seeing a subject in a small boat come from a dock and pull the net and take two fish out of it. The suspect was heading back to the dock about a block from my location. I parked my truck close to the house where the suspect would come out and headed for the stairway leading down to the water. I was just about there when the suspect came around the corner of the house carrying two steelhead.

I recognized the suspect as the one reported owning the net and selling the fish. He recognized me too and threw the two fish at me and started to run. I ducked under the fish and tackled him and hit my nose on one of the small trees in front of the house. The suspect jumped up and started running down the street, just out of arms reach, with me about three feet behind him. He was 6 feet and weighed about 180 pounds.

I was thinking about thumping him on the shoulder real hard with my five-cell flashlight but didn't. I told him as we ran, "I know who you are," and called him by name. I said, "You better stop, and let's get this over with." He turned as he ran and saw my nose bleeding and asked, "You're not going to arrest me for assault, are you?"

I said, "No, just for illegal netting."

He stopped, and I grabbed him by the arm and took him to my truck. I called the Seattle police, and they transported him to a juvenile detention facility for the night. He was fined $50 in juvenile court. My nose was broken, and I ended up with another black eye. Size still didn't matter in this patrol station.

We worked the fish ladder area again by boat the next week. Another officer and I were running without lights in his boat, and another boat driven by a poacher running without lights almost ran over us. We turned on our light, and the other boat took off trying to get away.

The suspect grounded his boat on the beach and took off running. Two other officers on the shore caught him. It was another one of the local juvenile poachers. The boat was stolen, so we confiscated the net he had in his boat and provided a case report to the juvenile authorities.

While we were processing the boat, radio dispatch advised that a net was found in the Snoqualmie River. I called a couple more officers working in another area and asked if they could assist us with the illegal net. We found the illegal gill net on a bend in the river along a back road. I assigned one car with two officers to sit on the south end of the road and the other car with two officers to watch the north end of the road.

Another officer, Kim Chandler, and I would sit in the bushes near the gill net with my portable radio and try to observe the poacher work the net and apprehend him. I parked my truck on another side road, and one of the other officers dropped Kim and me off by the net. It was real foggy, and the visibility was only about thirty feet. I saw a large stump beside the road near the net and told Kim to hide behind it. I was looking for a spot to hide on the other side of the net when I saw car headlights about one hundred feet away in the fog. I thought it was the other officer coming back. I asked on my portable radio, "What did you forget?" Then I realized it was the poachers and said, "They are here. Get ready." I didn't have anything to hide behind, so I dropped down on my back at the edge of the parking spot.

I raised my arm to cover my badge and keep it from shining in the headlights and covered my face with my sleeve. The car stopped about six feet away, and the driver got out and stood in the dark, four feet from my head. I was looking at him through the fingers of my hand just in case he started to take a whiz.

The driver said, "Okay," and three more subjects got out of the car and headed down to the net. The driver stood beside the open car door and watched. I could hear the water splashing as the three subjects pulled the net out of the river. I got up and quietly walked up to the driver and turned on my flashlight and said, "State wildlife agent. Don't nobody move." I reached into the car, shut the motor off, and took the keys.

I had my light shining on the three subjects down by the net and called for Kim to come and stand beside the driver. I walked closer to the river's edge when Kim had the driver under control and called the other officers to come on in, we had four subjects in custody. I told the three subjects down by the net to let me see their hands and come up real slow. The other cars arrived, and we obtained identification from the violators. They were tribal members from another area.

There wasn't any net season in the river, so they were cited for netting during the closed season. One of the violators had an outstanding warrant for his arrest and was transported and booked into jail. Kim and I finished pulling the net, which had caught two steelheads, and processed it for evidence. The four subjects appeared in court and were found guilty and fined $100 each.

I was riding with another officer, Jim Suda, in my detachment, patrolling the national forest for bear hunters near the old abandoned town of Lester in the Stampede Pass area. I had seen a black bear in that area earlier during the summer. We could hear hounds barking in the distance and headed that way. We found three trucks with dog boxes in the back, parked beside a large piece of timber between several clear-cuts.

The dogs were barking about two hundred yards above the road, and all the hunters were up in the woods. We parked behind the trucks and walked up into the timber and contacted the group of hunters. They were surprised to see us. There were six adult males with two teenaged boys and ten dogs standing under a fir tree with a 130-pound black bear twenty feet above the dogs.

One man was working on a Marlin lever-action rifle, and he said, "The kid was going to shoot the bear, and the rifle jammed." Two other men were standing off to one side of the tree with their rifles pointed up at the bear. The bear was just hanging on the side of the tree and was getting restless. The man working on the rifle hit the lever real hard with his hand. The action closed, and the rifle accidently discharged into the air.

The bear started coming down the tree, and one of the men with the rifles shot it. It fell to the ground, dead. I told the man, "Well, let me check your hunting license. I'll notch your tag for you, and we will be on our way."

The man produced a hunting license and said, "I already killed a bear this morning and don't have a tag."

I said, "Then why did you shoot this bear?"

He said, "Well, it was coming down, and I didn't want the dogs to get hurt."

I said, "You should have handed the rifle to the kid and let him shoot it or let the other hunter shoot it." I told him to drag the bear down to the trucks.

In the back of one of the trucks was another dead bear with the hunter's tag on it. The hunter gutted the bear while Jim issued him a citation for exceeding the limit on black bear. The bear was held for evidence, and the hunter forfeited $450 bail. The bear was donated to a charitable organization.

Over the years, the legislature would make new laws and make more work for the department and never provide any money for enforcement of the laws. We now had litter, ATV (all-terrain vehicles), and wood products laws to enforce. The regional agent's title was changed to captain, and then two positions opened after Lee Strickland retired. The department gave an oral test for the new positions and other officers, and I took it. I scored 88.6 and ended up fourth on the list for promotions.

A sheriff deputy (woods deputy) was assigned to the national forest to work on timber theft and off-road vehicle violations. On May 18 of 1980, I was riding with him, and we headed up the middle fork of the Snoqualmie River to check fishermen and for ATV violators. We signed in service on the radio, and radio dispatch advised that Mount Saint Helens had blown up and that it would be emergency traffic only for today. The deputy said, "I would like to see that. Let's see if we can get high enough to see anything."

We drove up to the top of a ridge west of Snoqualmie Pass and could look south and saw a big brown cloud of ash, dust, and smoke about sixty thousand feet in the air above the mountain. It was pretty in a way, but it had long-term effects on the state and the resources. A lot of the wildlife agents were required to assist with traffic control in the mountain area. The dust got into the carburetors of their vehicles and ruined the motors.

The rivers were damaged with the volume of mud and logs that had washed into the water. The roads and bridges in the area were washed out and destroyed. A large amount of timber had been blown down, and the ash in some areas was over five inches deep.

Later that year, the wildlife biologist in our region wanted to do a mountain goat study in the Cascade Mountains portion of my patrol district. Bob Overly and I volunteered to help him. We would drive as close as we could to the mountainous area the goats inhabited and then hike for about six miles along the ridge and camp overnight to count all the goats we observed.

The biologist didn't have room in his vehicle for the three of us to ride, so I drove my truck. The biologist would drive my truck back to the forest service office and go home in his own vehicle. Larry would drive another road system the next afternoon and pick Bob and me up at around 4:00 pm.

About two miles from the end of the dead-end road system, the right front tire on my truck went flat. I took the Hi-Lift jack to raise the front wheel off the ground while Bob started to loosen the lug nuts to take the wheel off. The biologist went into the back of my truck to get the spare tire. He threw it out of the truck, instead of handing it to one of us, and it took one bounce and bounced down the steep mountainside for what sounded like a half mile. Nobody said biologists were smart!

I looked at him and said, "Go get it." He never found it. I called another officer working in North Bend and asked if he could bring the spare tire off his truck to us so my truck would be able to get back to town. Bob and I started hiking from my disabled truck, and the biologist waited for the other officer to arrive with the spare tire. Bob and I each carried a backpack with food, water, and sleeping bags.

We had a tent to keep from getting wet in the event it rained during the night. After our freeze-dried dinner, we built a small campfire and enjoyed the clear night in the mountains. We put the fire out before crawling into the tent and going to bed. When we woke up at daylight, we found a light dusting of ash all over our tent and backpacks.

At first we thought the fire had started back up during the night and the ash had drifted onto our tent. We then saw the ash had covered all the surrounding brush and knew that Mount Saint Helens had blown up again. The volcano had been quiet for a spell but, once again, had started spewing out ash all over the state. It coated our arms and clothes as we walked, and we had to put our handkerchiefs over our nose and mouth so we could breathe.

We saw one black bear and counted the few mountain goats that we saw, and Larry picked us up as planned. It was a good hike and a change of pace from arresting poachers. We didn't see many goats and recommended that the number of goat permits in that unit be reduced for the following year.

Larry wanted to do an overnight patrol in the big twenty-five foot boat up in the San Juan Islands in the northern part of our region. He wanted me to go with him to assist in checking other boats. We took some food for our meals and sleeping bags to sleep in on the bunks under the bow. There just happened to be a crab pot aboard to sample the crab population for the biologist while we anchored in a cove that night. I must report that the crab population tasted good in that area and should be able to sustain additional harvest in the future!

The next day was sunny and clear and the water was flat as we were heading back to Seattle and I was driving the boat. Larry was trying to help navigate by reading the charts. He couldn't read the small print and asked, "What does that say?" I looked down to read the chart and hit a six-inch log about four feet long in the water. It bent one of the twin propellers.

The propellers vibrated so bad we had to run slow. Larry started complaining about my driving and hitting the piece of log. I said if he would wear his glasses, I wouldn't have to look away from the water. We docked in a marina close by, in Anacortes, and spent another night on the boat and had the propellers repaired the next day and headed home.

The last day of elk season, I was waiting by a hunter's truck in the dark outside the Cedar River Watershed gate near North Bend. I could hear someone walking on the rocks, and I could smell blood. I identified myself and shined my flashlight on the ground at his feet as he approached so he could see where he was walking and I could see how many people were coming back to the truck.

A single hunter was returning to the truck, and I could see blood on both of his pants legs and one white hair on the center of his shirt. I asked to check his license, and the hunter produced a valid license and an unnotched elk tag. I asked if he killed anything, and he replied no. I asked him about the blood on his pants, and when I picked the hair off his shirt, he said he killed a three-point.

I kept looking at the white hair as I was about to write him a citation for failing to notch his elk tag. The more I looked at it; it didn't look like an elk hair. I said, "This doesn't look like an elk hair. I think you shot a deer."

He replied, "Yes, it was a three-point deer." Deer season was closed, so I wrote him a citation for killing a deer during the closed season and held the deer hair and his rifle for evidence.

I told him to meet me back there tomorrow morning and we would go retrieve the deer or I would also charge him with wastage of a big game animal. I was lucky to be in the right place at the right time again!

The next morning, Commadore Mann, a USFW agent, rode along with me to meet the poacher. It was real foggy, so I told Commadore to wait by the radio at the truck and give me directions if I got lost. I took my portable radio, and the poacher and I headed up the mountain to get the deer. We found the three-point blacktail buck deer lying in a small clearing at the top of the mountain.

I cut it in half so we would have an easier time carrying it through the brush, back to the truck. The poacher started off to my right, and I asked, "Where you going?"

He said, "Back to the truck."

I said, "The truck is this way," and pointed to the left. We argued, so I called Commadore on the radio and asked him to take the .30-30 rifle behind the truck seat and fire it into a tree. The two shots came from my left, so we headed in that direction. It was getting foggier, and the poacher kept drifting off to the right as we headed back down the mountain.

Before we got back to the truck, the poacher wore out and said he couldn't go any farther. So I carried the hindquarters on my shoulder and pulled the front half of the deer by the antlers. I thought I was going to have to carry the poacher too and had to have Commadore fire the rifle two more times before we got back to the truck. A lesson learned was to take a compass and plenty of help to retrieve evidence.

A lot of police officers would tell me they wouldn't want my job checking hunters with loaded gun and knifes. I would tell them at least I knew they had guns and was on the alert when I approached them. I wasn't afraid to check hunters with loaded guns, but I still had nightmares about getting shot at and of my pistol never firing back.

One night I dreamed I was in a drugstore checking hunting license stubs when two men walked in and said, "This is a holdup." One man pointed a pistol at me, and I drew my pistol and shot him in the chest. This time my pistol went off, and the bullet made a big six-inch hole in his chest. He pointed his pistol at me again, and I shot him again in the chest, I woke up in a cold sweat. I guess my subconscious mind knew how dangerous a wildlife officer's job could be.

My marriage was on the rocks, and I was pretty depressed. I was taking counseling and asked the therapist what he could do for me. He said, "Well, I can be your friend." I said if that was all he could do for me, I could talk to other friends that didn't charge me $60 an hour. I made up my mind to only think about the good things in life and never went back.

MOVE TO OMAK

I got divorced in the spring of 1981, learned to cook, and lived happily ever after. I transferred over to the Okanogan station in Eastern Washington that was vacant since the officer retired. My new patrol detachment would include Okanogan County, Douglas County, and part of Grant County. It was about 100 miles wide at the widest part and 120 miles long and included the Pasayten Wilderness. It started at the Canadian border and went south to the city of East Wenatchee on the Columbia River. I would also get my first four-wheel drive truck but no air-conditioning.

I would live in Omak, a town of three thousand people, and supervise five wildlife agents and two wildlife control agents and do more real game warden work managing the wildlife resources. The region 2 office was 150 miles away in Ephrata, so we would hold mini region meetings for the north half in the large room of the Omak fish hatchery. It was part of my responsibility to coordinate meetings with the public and department personnel on season and rule changes.

Eastern Washington has a lot more wildlife resource and fewer people than I was used to working with in the Seattle area. Okanogan County is the biggest in the state but only had about 50,000 people in eight small towns as compared to King County with 1,500,000 people in Seattle. All the hunters and fishermen would come over from the west side of the mountains on opening day and stay up to a week recreating.

There were game birds, white-tailed deer, mule deer, bighorn sheep, mountain goats, mountain lions, black bears, and moose; and the lakes had good trout populations. The hatchery manager, Ken Woodward, and his wife, Pauline, were very nice and made my working there a real pleasure. The fish and wildlife biologist and wildlife area managers were easy to work with too.

Since this was a more rural area, the officers and I worked with the other law enforcement agencies and knew them on a first-name basis for arrest assist and on searches. This part of the state had a lot of national forest and public lands and included large cattle ranches and apple orchards.

The deer would migrate over twenty-two miles out of the mountains in the winter when the snow was too deep to walk in, and they created a lot of damage for the orchardist and to the haystacks of the ranchers. Beavers would also cut down a lot of apple trees along the Okanogan River. We would assist the biologist in the winter and spring with deer surveys by hiking down the mountain for about six miles and counting all the deer we saw.

The lakes in this region had a lot of trout in them, and all the fishermen would catch over their limits of fish. So we would hold check stations for about the first two weeks of fishing season. I had to take eight hours of traffic-flagging training to be certified to direct vehicles from the highway into our check stations. We wrote a lot of over-limit tickets and seized a lot of trout. They were donated to the county jail.

I never profiled fishermen or hunters as every boat or group would be different. Violators have a way of looking guilty by their actions, the way they held their fishing rod, or by fishing in secluded places with their head turning, looking for the warden.

I would keep track of the number of people I checked each day and how many arrests I made. I would arrest about one out of every twenty people I checked. In Seattle, I could drive around all the little lakes, and if I didn't recognize having checked the person before, I would check them and arrest them. I could come back in two hours, and there would be a new group of people. I would arrest one out of ten. Okanogan was too big to drive around the lakes every two hours, but there were plenty of lakes to check.

The fish biologist wanted me to help him plant fingerling trout. The hatchery truck was being used in another part of the state, and he wanted me to put the fish tank in the back of my pickup. I suggested that we tie it in. He said it was heavy enough to stay in. We loaded it with water and trout and took off for a couple lakes. We unloaded over half of the fish in the first lake and had to stop at a gate before going up the hill to the second lake. I thought I heard a noise when I pulled through the gate and looked in my rearview mirror.

The tank had slid back off the truck and sat in the middle of the road. The biologist looked at me and said, "Don't say it." We had to borrow some plastic garbage cans to put the fish in and took them to the lake before they died. After we dumped the water out of the tank, we could lift it back into the truck.

The department had a horse and three mules for back-country patrols. The officer in the Methow Valley, Sig Bakke, had his own horses, and he would take one to ride and pack the mules to carry the tent and food for patrols in the Pasayten Wilderness. I would ride the state horse or the white mule.

We would ride around and check the high lakes and always seemed behind the fishermen or to arrive before they started fishing. I suggested we each stay at a lake and let the fishermen come to us. Three of us packed in and stayed at different lakes for two days and checked more fishermen and made a lot more arrests for no license and over limits.

Sig and I were going on a pack trip into the mountains shortly after Claude Dallas, the notorious Idaho game warden killer, escaped from jail. There was an alert bulletin sent out to all law enforcement detachments stating he might be heading through Washington to Canada and may be going through the Methow Valley. Sig and I discussed it and went into town to buy groceries.

We passed a subject as we were coming out of a store who gave Sig a funny look. Sig was in uniform, but I was in plain clothes and not wearing a sidearm. Sig and I looked at each other and I asked, "What was that all about? Did you arrest him for something?"

Sig said, "I never saw him before. He is a stranger in town." He kinda matched Dallas's size and age.

Sig went to his truck to look at the alert bulletin for a physical description while I stayed on the street keeping track of the subject. Sig came back and said, "He is about the same size. What are we going to do?" I told Sig to stay a short distance behind me and I would follow the subject. When we were in an area that would not endanger other people, I would identify myself and badge him, and then Sig was to come up for backup.

The subject didn't appear to be armed but had a loose shirt on over his belt and could have a gun hidden under it. The subject went behind the store in the parking lot, and I got within three feet of him and showed him my badge. I said, "Sir, there is an arrest warrant for a person who matches your description," and asked if he had any identification. I was ready to jump on him if he went for a gun or jump out of the way if the shooting started. He had an Oregon driver's license, and his eyes were a different color. I was disappointed it wasn't Dallas as he was still free.

We worked the Pasayten Wilderness area again in September during the high hunt for deer. My old horse would wear out riding in, so I would let it rest and ride the white mule checking hunters. The mule was so stubborn; it would hold the bit in its mouth and keep on walking straight even with its head pulled to one side. My spurs didn't seem to bother him either, but I surprised a lot of hunters and fishermen riding him.

I was riding the white mule checking hunters one afternoon and saw a man in the willows down by a stream. He would stand up and look around and then duck back down. I had an orange vest over my uniform and looked like a hunter and rode up to him before he figured out who I was. He was cleaning a large stringer of trout. I identified myself and said, "Looks like you have a few over your limit. Do you have a fishing license?"

He produced a fishing license and started complaining. He said, "I am the unluckiest person in the world. I got arrested for DUI last year, and the court took my driver's license away. My car was parked across the street from my house, so I got in and parked it in front of my house and was arrested for driving without a license. Now I am miles back in the wilderness with a lot of fish, and who would ride up but the game warden."

He had been fishing to catch enough trout for a fish fry for the hunting camp. He needed more than eight trout for the four hunters, so he caught sixteen, two times over his daily limits. I wrote him a citation and seized eight of the trout for evidence. It was cold and snowed the whole time we were camped in the mountains, so the trout didn't spoil and were donated to the jail when we returned to civilization.

Another officer and I had snowmobiles stored at the hatchery to use in the winter to check mountain lion hunters and assist with search and rescue. A biologist would trap and collar lynx on a sixty-mile trap line to study their movement in the winter. He had to ride a snowmobile to set and check the padded traps every day, and it was too dangerous to be out there all alone.

Other officers and I would take turns and ride with him. We would start at 6:00 am and get back to the truck after dark; it was a long day bouncing up and down on the rough trails. If a person stepped off the snowmobile, they would sink up to their armpits in the soft snow.

**Checking lynx traps in the North Cascade
Mountains with a wildlife biologist**

One day I was checking out my snowmobile to get it ready for a day on the trap line. I rode it up to a frozen lake to see if anyone was fishing illegally. I was all alone, and nobody was there. So I walked out on the ice, and I stomped on it. It appeared to be over six inches thick. I rode my snowmobile out on the ice to check out some chucks of ice where I thought someone had cut a hole and fished in the past week.

Riding out on the center of the lake, the ice looked a dark blue as if the water was awfully close to the surface. I headed my snowmobile toward shore and got off and walked about twenty yards and stomped real hard. My heel went through the three-fourth-inch ice, and it surprised me so bad I let out a loud yell and ran back to the snowmobile and got off the lake. It was too cold to go swimming, and it would have been hard to explain why my snowmobile was on the bottom of the lake. Other people lose snowmobiles in lakes every year.

It was spring, and I was on a day off. The biologist and the wildlife control officer, John Danielson, were checking the lynx trap line. They came to my house around 11:00 am and wanted me to help them get a bear cub out of one of the traps. They had gone there earlier, but the sow (female bear) was running around and they couldn't get close enough to release the cub. I asked how big the clearing was with the trap and cub.

They said, "Pretty big, about fifty yards long." They wanted me to stand guard with a shotgun while they turned the cub loose. I told them I would go, but if the sow got within twenty-five yards of me, I would shoot it. When we arrived back at the trap, I found the clearing to be very small, fifteen by twenty-five yards, with low brush all around it. The sow was nowhere in sight.

I told them the plan had changed. As soon as I saw the sow in the clearing, I would shoot it; I didn't want anyone to get hurt. I walked in, and they followed me up to the squalling bear cub pulling on the trap chain. I said, "Okay, get it out." I was turning and looking all around when I heard the sow coming in the brush. I looked down, and they still didn't have the cub loose. I said, "Hurry up, she's coming." The sow entered the clearing, and they both took off running. So I thought the cub was loose.

Backing up, I saw the tranquilizer gun lying on the ground and the bear cub running past it with the catch pole still on it neck.

The cub ran and climbed up a nearby tree, and the little sow came charging at me. It was now about twenty yards away, and I kept backing up but didn't shoot. It growled and stopped by the tree. It made a bluff charge and then climbed up the tree behind the cub.

I turned around and saw John standing behind me with his pistol drawn. He said, "I was going to shoot, but I thought if Bud didn't shoot, I wouldn't either." I told him it was a good thing he didn't shoot as I thought they were long gone and that gun going off beside me would have made me mess my pants! We tranquilized the sow—she only weighed about eighty pounds—and the biologist climbed the tree and caught the bear cub to take the catch pole off it. Everyone lived happily ever after.

I received a complaint of two fishermen on Conconully Lake taking over their limit of trout. I was on a day off, so I drove my personal van and parked near the suspect's cabin to wait and watch. In the past years two, old men had been caught with seven hundred trout from the lake. The daily limit is eight trout, and I observed two men in a boat take over two times the limit of fish into the cabin and then go back out on the lake and start fishing again, catching and keeping more fish.

They came back in with more trout. But I didn't know how many people were in the cabin, so I didn't contact them. The prosecutor in the county was pretty hard to get along with and wouldn't issue a search warrant unless you had the case 99.9 percent solved. He would worry about his conviction record. I waited until the suspects loaded their car with a large bag of fish and headed home. I followed them home and contacted the prosecutor the next morning to obtain a search warrant.

The prosecutor asked, "What is the address of the house you want to search?" I opened his office door and said, "See that white house across the street? That's it." I had the suspects' names and description of the property and was issued a search warrant. John and I searched the house and arrested the two men for forty-five trout over their limit. They each forfeited $275 bail.

Wildlife agent Bill Hebner received a poaching complaint of an old moonshiner killing a deer during the closed season. It was reported years ago that a bear had fallen into his whiskey mash barrel and got drunk and stumbled around the area for a few days before the alcohol wore off. We contacted the reporting party and checked the field where the violation took place. Next to his field, in the suspect's field, was a large pine tree, a "skinning tree" with a rope and pulley hanging on a limb and eight fresh deer legs, sawed off at the hock, lying under it.

We contacted the prosecutor and obtained a search warrant and took the liquor control agent and two sheriff deputies along with three of us wildlife officers to search the residence. Two officers would secure the residence, two officers would secure the evidence and, two officers would do the searching.

The suspect was home, and I advised him we were there to search his house, barn, and vehicles and handed him a copy of the search warrant. He stood in the doorway and refused to let us in. A deputy was holding the screen door open, I was standing in front of the suspect, and Bill was standing next to me holding a clipboard. After about five minutes, I whispered to Bill to put the clipboard down and said, "He's coming out."

I grabbed the suspect's arm and pulled him out and threw him on the porch floor. He was screaming, "You're breaking my arm." I replied, "Then don't resist," and we cuffed him and put him in the deputy's car. We found a loaded .44 Mag pistol just above his head on a shelf above the door. We found two boxes full of fresh-wrapped meat in the freezer with deer and the month and date written on them. Parts of an old whiskey still were found in his barn but were not seized.

I went out to the car and asked the suspect when he shot those deer and he said, "Last year."

I replied, "Then why did you write this month's date on them?" He just grunted. We found hip bones from two different deer in the frozen packages. The suspect was charged with two counts of possession of deer during the closed season. He appeared in court and requested a jury trial. He said a Colville Indian gave him that deer meat. The jury didn't believe him. He was found guilty and fined $500   .

Bill received another poaching complaint in early fall, and we went back in the woods to contact the suspect living in a small log cabin. When we knocked on the door, I recognized the young man as one of the juvenile snaggers that was always in trouble when I worked in the Seattle area. I said, "Hello, John, what you doing over here?"   He said, "I live here with my mom and stepdad." We told John and his mother that we were investigating a deer-poaching complaint. John was no longer a juvenile. I asked if he had been shooting any deer, and he said no. On the toe of his shoe was a big round drop of fresh dried blood, and I pointed to it and said, "You better start telling the truth." He started getting real nervous, and after a few more questions, he admitted helping his stepdad shoot and gut the deer.

The doe deer carcass was hanging in a root cellar behind the house. Bill and I seized the skinned deer carcass, and Bill issued a citation to John and his stepdad for killing a deer during the closed season. They came to court and were found guilty and fined $350 each.

The regional manager, Ray Duff; Bill; and I were working spotlighters the first night of deer season. Bill and Ray were in Bill's vehicle, and I was by myself. We contacted a truck with the driver shining a light out the driver's window. He had a loaded rifle on the seat beside him. He said he had hunted all day and didn't see any deer, so he was looking for one on his way back to camp.

Bill issued him a citation for hunting big game with an artificial light, and I transported him to jail. He said he wasn't feeling good and didn't want to go to jail. He wasn't talking much, and about halfway to the jail, he started shaking and threw his head back on the seat with his eyes closed. I thought maybe he was faking a heart attack since suspects had been reported to do that. I watched him for a few minutes and saw he was breathing normally and wasn't complaining anymore.

Bill and Ray were following behind me, and I advised them, "I think he went to sleep." And then the suspect appeared to move, listening to me. I passed a direction sign to the hospital and asked the suspect if he always hunted by himself, and he opened his eyes and saw the sign and said no. He didn't ask to go to the hospital, so I took him straight to jail and booked him. The next day he appeared before the judge and pled guilty and was fined $450. I asked the judge if he complained about having any health problems, and he said "No, he was just mad about being booked into jail."

Bill received another report of someone snaring deer during the closed season. We checked the area and found where a snare had been tied and the ground was all torn up with lots of deer tracks and hair lying all around. The suspect was reportedly living in a small cabin at the end of the road. We knocked on the door, but no one answered. We went around to the back of the cabin and yelled, "Is anybody here?" No one answered.

We observed a fresh deer hide lying on the roof, so we went back around to the front of the house and were going to wait in our truck for the suspect to return home. I could see a man through the front window walk in through the back door of the cabin; we never did know where he came from. We knocked on the front door again and asked him about the deer hide. He had another dried and stretched deer hide in the cabin and some dried deer meat but wouldn't admit to snaring the deer.

He was a hippie from Ohio and had a warrant for his arrest for DUI, so I took him to jail. When I was booking him, I found a deer snare in his coat pocket with deer hair on it. I charged him with possession of deer during the closed season. He was found guilty and given a thirty-day jail sentence. He told the judge there was a hindquarter of deer meat lying under a wheelbarrow behind the woodpile. Bill and I returned to his cabin and retrieved the evidence before it spoiled.

I was issued a new patrol vehicle: a blue Chevrolet Blazer with a black top and no air-conditioning. I was in charge of the budget for my patrol districts. My supervisor said it was okay, so I had the top painted white. At least it would be a little cooler in the summer. I received a title name change to sergeant, and we were allowed to have undercover license plates on our vehicles, without any department decals.

It was early October, and I was driving through Wenatchee on my way home from firearm instructor training in Olympia. I heard wildlife agent Rick Peterson giving directions to other officers about illegal hunting. I asked if he needed assistance. He said yes. I crossed over the Columbia River and contacted him and two other officers trying to find some closed season hunters down in the coulee from Waterville.

An abandoned railroad track ran through the middle of the valley, and the poachers were reported to be on a speeder work cart and shooting chukar partridge along the tracks. They had checked both ends of the valley and couldn't locate the suspects. We all piled into my Blazer, and I straddled the rails and drove up the tracks in an attempt to locate them heading back to their house. We heard shooting come from behind us.

We backed up to the road crossing and were about to drive south when we saw four men on the speeder cart coming in our direction. I was the only person in plain clothes, so I parked on the tracks and got out and raised the hood on my vehicle as if I was having motor trouble. The driver of the speeder cart, a known poacher, stopped about a hundred yards from us and shut the motor off and waited. They were starting to get nervous and were going to leave and go back down the tracks.

I yelled at the other officers to come on, and we all ran toward the cart. The man couldn't get the motor started and I yelled, "State wildlife agent! Hold it!" We were able to catch them with their shotguns loaded and with a half-dozen chukars in a lunch box. They were all arrested for hunting chukar during the closed season and for possession of a loaded gun on a motor-driven vehicle. Their shotguns were seized along with the cart for evidence. The owner of the speeder cart was a known poacher and forfeited bail. His shotgun and the speeder cart were confiscated by the court.

About midnight on a cold frosty night, I received a telephone call from another wildlife agent. He said he and another officer were hunting grouse in Okanogan County on their day off and were going to stay in Bill's house for the night. Bill had gone out to cut some firewood with a state trooper that day and had not returned home.

I advised the officer that if Bill didn't return by morning, I would come and help look for them.

Bill didn't return that night, so the three of us piled into my vehicle. I drove to a place where I thought Bill might go to cut firewood. We found Bill's truck loaded with cut and split firewood. The windows on the truck were rolled down, and Bill's long-sleeve flannel shirt was lying on the ground beside the truck. A chain saw, gas can, and ax were also lying there.

We looked around and couldn't find any blood to indicate he or the trooper were injured or any tire tracks of another vehicle being there. The trooper's wife had also called the state patrol office about her missing husband, and the sergeant had the state plane up looking for the trooper. I gave the sergeant the location of Bill's truck for an aerial search with the plane.

About a half hour after we found Bill's truck, the sergeant in the plane spotted Bill and the trooper walking on a road back to the truck. I had driven to another road and was blowing the horn on my vehicle, hoping they would hear it and know someone was looking for them. Bill and the trooper were back at his truck when we arrived back there.

Bill and the trooper were only wearing T-shirts and jeans and were pretty cold. They were both embarrassed, and the story went like this: Bill said they finished cutting the load of firewood, and deer season was open. Bill had his rifle, and it was still an hour until dark. So they decided to hunt uphill from the truck. It was warm, so he left his long-sleeve shirt by the truck. In a short time, they spotted a buck, and Bill shot and wounded it.

They followed the buck for over a half mile and couldn't find it. So they headed back to the truck but got lost. It got dark, and they tried to build a fire by tearing up Bill's hunting license and some dollar bills from his wallet. They didn't have matches, so they tried to start the fire by shooting at it with the .30-06 rifle, hoping the fire from the muzzle flash would catch the paper on fire. It didn't!

It was pretty steep country. They didn't want to stumble around in the dark and fall off a cliff, so they decided to stay where they were until morning. It got real cold, and they hugged each other all night to keep warm. When daylight came, they could see which direction to go and were headed back to the truck when they heard the plane flying overhead.

The next fall, I saw the trooper in the patrol office and said, "I see you saved the state a lot of money this year." The trooper asked "How did I do that?" I said, "By not going hunting and getting lost." He didn't think it was very funny.

The orchardists in Okanogan County hire a lot of migrant workers to pick their fruit and then have them prune the trees in the winter. A lot of them were undocumented and killed a lot of deer to eat and then send the money they earn home to Mexico. Bill received another deer-poaching complaint about pickers in an orchard up at Orville next to the Canadian border.

We went to the cabin and saw a dog chewing on a fresh deer leg. Several men sitting in front of the cabin got up and went into the cabin when we stopped. That was a stroke of luck for us as most illegal migrants scatter like a flock of quail when law enforcement pull into an orchard, and the chase is on.

We went to the door and questioned them about killing deer. We could see some fried meat in a skillet on the stove and asked what it was. They couldn't say the English word for deer but could understand better English than we could understand Spanish. We said, "Deer," and asked to see inside their refrigerator. They opened it, and we saw a brown paper sack of fresh deer meat and deer hair frozen solid in the freezer box.

None of the eight Hispanic males had a valid green card. We called the border patrol, and they arrived and took all of them and deported them back to Mexico. We had a hard time cutting the frozen deer meat out of the freezer box. That summer, Bill transferred over to region 4, and the Tonasket station was vacant during the deer season. I was getting a lot of complaints all winter and working long hours. Nothing ever changes!

In 1984, the Supreme Court decided that officers needed to advise the dumb crooks that they had the right to an attorney. The court would also appoint one for them if they couldn't afford one. We also had to tell the crooks they didn't have to say anything that might incriminate themselves, as if they weren't smart enough to figure that one out.

In past years, we had a standard form printed and would attempt to get a written statement about the facts of the violation. Most courts wouldn't allow the statement to be entered into evidence, but if a suspect signed a statement, he was more apt to stick to the facts if they later came into court.

After getting home from working all day, an orchardist called and reported hearing a rifle shot in his orchard just before dark. I told him it would be too dark to find anybody by the time it took me to get there. I would be there the first thing in the morning. I called John and asked if he could go with me tomorrow. He said he could and would pick me up before 7:00 am.

We arrived just after daylight at the orchard and found two young men pruning apple trees. We asked them if they had been working there the day before, and they said yes. They were very nervous but denied hearing any shot at dark. They let us check the trunk of their car, and it was clean. So we drove on through the orchard. I told John they sure seemed guilty.

John said maybe it was because he had arrested one of them for killing a bighorn sheep a couple months ago. We came around a corner in the orchard and saw some ravens fly up from two fresh boned-out deer carcasses lying on the snow. John said, "What are we going to do?"

I said, "Stop at the first picker cabin we come to and knock on the door."

The orchardist didn't pay the pickers after the apple harvest but let them stay in the cabins so they would be available to prune trees in January. The pickers generally lived off the land during the downtime, and deer meat was high on the menu.

We came around another corner in the orchard and found a cabin. We stopped, and in the front yard and on the snow was fresh blood. I knocked on the door, and a Hispanic male with blood all over his pant legs opened the door. We had another language problem. So we called the border patrol again, and they came to interpret for us. They took the two suspects to the city jail for questioning, and we followed in John's truck.

John said that a couple years earlier, he and the hatchery manager caught a couple Hispanics poaching. The hatchery manager told the suspects, "You are going to the county jail."

John said, "They don't understand you."

The hatchery manager said, a little louder, "You are going to the county jail."

John again said, "They still don't understand you."

The hatchery manager said, real slow and real loud, "You are going to go to the county jail." They still didn't understand but went to jail.

Halfway to town, I saw a raven fly up from a dump beside the road. A set of big truck-tire tracks stopped at a cable gate, and two subjects got out and walked in the fresh snow. I told John to stop. About ten feet inside the cable lay a dead mule deer doe. It was shot once through the ribs and field dressed and dumped without any of the meat taken. I took a photo of the tire tracks and the deer, and then we continued on into town.

The two suspects in jail admitted to killing two deer in another area and dumping the carcasses that we saw near their cabin. They had the deer meat in another cabin, so we went to retrieve it. They both were documented workers, so we cited them for killing two deer during the closed season and booked them into jail. They were each found guilty and given a thirty-day jail sentence.

As John and I were heading home, I told him I would find out who dumped that dead doe. He couldn't work with me the next day, so I parked at the edge of town along the road leading to the dump and looked at all the wide truck tires that went past me. At noon, a gray Chevrolet truck with wide tires and a rifle in the rack in the rear window went past me. The tire tread matched the tire tracks left in the snow by the dead doe.

I followed the truck to a house at the edge of town. It was the nervous subject in the orchard that John had arrested for killing the bighorn. He got out and walked into the house before I could contact him. I parked behind his truck and glanced into the bed of the truck as I walked past it going to the door. It looked awfully clean, as if someone had washed it. I asked the suspect to come to my Blazer and advised him of his Miranda rights and told him I wanted to talk to him about the deer he had in his truck and dumped along the side of the road. Think positive!

He said, "Oh!" and I knew I had the right person. Most times, one just has to ask the right questions. He admitted shooting the deer with his buddy at dark a couple days earlier. It was the shot the orchardist reported.

They were going to sell the deer to another man for $100. After they killed it, the third person didn't want the deer, so they took it up the road and dumped it by the dump with the cable gate. They were both arrested for killing a deer during the closed season and for wastage of a game animal. They both forfeited $725 in court.

I was contacting the third subject about buying the deer, and he said he never told them to shoot any deer for him. As I was questioning him, I received a call from radio dispatch advising me about poaching in progress, so I left. He was not charged. The Sinlahekin Wildlife Area manager, Gordon, called about someone spotlighting in front of his house. It was about fifteen miles away, so I headed in that direction. I arrived and contacted Gordon on the road, at the entrance to his driveway.

A station wagon car was parked just off the road with the lights on. Gordon said he saw the car go by and someone spotlighted the fields. It stopped at his driveway, and he heard several shots and saw several men moving around the car. He went out to the road and found the car with the doors open and the motor running and a loaded .22 rimfire rifle lying on the front seat. A live white-tailed deer fawn was standing in the back seat of the car and another dead doe deer was lying on the ground beside the car. He said he took the rifle and shut the door so the fawn couldn't get out and shut the motor off.

About that time, two Hispanic men came up dragging a third deer, and when they saw him, they took off running down the valley toward town. The fawn died in the car while we were talking. I told Gordon to wait by the car and I would go down the valley and see if I could contact the men that ran. I drove up and down the road a couple times with my siren blaring and shining my spotlight on the creek. I told them to come out or I would turn my dog loose. Then I shut off my lights and drove back down the valley and waited by a narrow spot on the road by a cliff. It was a bright moonlit night. It was cold, and the frozen snow crunched when someone walked on it.

About a half hour after I shut off my lights, I heard someone walking toward my location. I got out of my vehicle and waited until the person was close to me. I shined my flashlight on him and said "State wildlife agent, come here." He was a Hispanic male, so I searched him and took a knife away from him and placed him in the front seat and questioned him about the car and dead deer. He said he was in the car but didn't own it.

A short time later, two more men came walking in the snow. I took my keys out of the ignition and told the first suspect to be quiet and stepped out of my vehicle. I contacted the two men and placed them in front of my vehicle and searched them. They were two more Hispanic males from the car. Nobody would admit to owning the car, so I drove back to have Gordon identify them. He couldn't believe my luck; he identified the last two subjects I contacted. I was in the right spot again.

I called for a vehicle impound and had the car towed. There weren't any other officers working at that end of the county. I didn't have enough handcuffs, so I took the three men, without handcuffs and sitting behind me, to jail. It was not a very safe practice to do alone. I turned my rearview mirror so I could see the two behind me and drove to the jail.

Gordon gutted the deer for evidence, and later they were donated to the jail. The three subjects were found guilty and given thirty days in jail. I never found the owner of the car, but a lady paid the tow bill and retrieved the car a month later. I had a very busy three days and made nine big game arrests.

A rancher east of Tonasket called and reported that his neighbor killed one of his pigs and two deer. John and I went to investigate the deer poaching. We found the abandoned trailer the man reported and found blood all over the inside of the kitchen and bathtub. The suspect lived a half mile up the road from the trailer. The road was snowed in for the winter. So John and I carried my portable, and we walked in on foot.

A small twenty-foot-by-twenty-foot stick log cabin about six feet high sat at the end of the road by an open hay shed. We knocked on the door, and a black man came to the door. Four people lived there: two men, a woman, and a teenage boy. The second man was so dirty we thought he was a black man too. We identified ourselves and said we were investigating the deer poaching. They denied killing any deer.

The man said he had some pork hanging in the shed but no deer. As we walked to the shed, I could see a couple fresh deer hides hanging on the fence. There were a dozen quarters of meat hanging in the shed. I showed John the deer hides and told him to go get the deer meat hanging in the shed. He asked, "Which deer? That's pig." I said, "The small quarters are deer." We looked inside the cabin to see if there was any more meat in it.

The cabin had a dirt floor with a wood-burning stove, one chair, a double-size mattress lying on the dirt, and an old-style kitchen sink and a table. A five-gallon bucket used for a toilet sat by the door. I was afraid I would get lice from being there. I told the people there were food stamp programs, welfare, and other means to get food in this day and age without stealing and poaching. I told the two men they would be arrested.

I contacted radio dispatch to check for warrants on the two men. The older black male had a $650 warrant for DUI. John issued a citation to the younger male for possession of deer during the closed season. The older male was cited then transported to be booked into jail on the DUI warrant. Both men came to court and were found guilty and sentenced to thirty days in jail. I don't know if they were ever charged with killing their neighbor's hog.

A captain position opened up in the Spokane Region, and my name was next in line on the personnel list. The personnel department called me and asked if I wanted a promotion. I said I would go and talk to the regional supervisor and see if I wanted to move. When I started working back in 1965, I always worked hard at being the best field officer I could be and thought someday I would like to be a law supervisor.

I was considering taking the promotion as working in a small town had its disadvantages. Everybody knew everybody's business. I couldn't even go to church on my day off to relax and worship the good Lord without someone bitching to me about the game department or the hunting seasons.

I had just built a new house and finished the landscaping. I would have a hard time recovering my investment from a quick sale of the house. My salary would not increase very much, and I would have to supervise over twice as many officers. I would be another 150 miles farther away from my family and friends. After considering all my options, I turned the promotion down.

An officer quit, leaving the Brewster station in my detachment vacant, and another officer, Dale Svedberg, transferred into the vacant Tonasket station. Dale received a poaching complaint the night before deer season advising that a deer was hanging in a camp close to the Canadian border. We arrived just after daylight and found a truck and camping trailer parked beside a small creek. A skinned carcass of a doe deer was hanging in a tree nearby. It was stiff, and the skin was starting to dry. It had definitely not been killed during legal hunting hours.

We knocked on the door of the trailer and found the owner sleeping inside. He invited us in, and we questioned him about the deer in the tree. He wouldn't admit to shooting the deer. He had a valid license and deer tag, and it was the first morning of deer season. It seemed kinda unusual that he wouldn't be hunting with his buddies. We were able to contact one of his buddies and questioned him about the deer.

The second subject was very nervous and knew more than he was telling. It appeared the deer was shot on the way to the hunting camp, but he was afraid of his buddy in the trailer and wouldn't say who shot it. We went back to the trailer and saw a little dried blood and a deer hair in the open bed of the truck. When investigating wildlife crimes, it isn't as easy as on TV.

A wildlife officer doesn't have the best place or conditions to question a suspect nor have all the tools and equipment needed to collect all the trace evidence like they do on CSI. We seized the deer hair, the deer carcass, and the fresh hide for evidence and issued a citation for possession of a doe deer during the closed season to the subject in the trailer, the owner of the truck. The blood sample was too small to collect.

The defendant did not appear in court and wrote a nasty letter to the judge. The defendant said he was not going to appear in a kangaroo court and called us the judge's henchmen. He said we threatened to kill him and were going to make it look like a hunting accident. The judge issued an arrest warrant for his arrest. The defendant wrote another letter to the WGD office in Olympia threatening to sue for $5,000,000 but would forget all about it if they paid him $1,000,000.

The defendant lived on the west side of the state and never came to court and the warrant was never served. Over a year later, I was riding with two other officers on Interstate 90 and heading home from a training class in Olympia. We were in uniform, and as we passed a car, I looked out the window. Driving the car beside us was the deer poacher with a small child riding with him. He looked out his window and saw me looking at him, and he got a real sick look on his face.

My buddy pulled up behind him and turned on the red light and siren, but he wouldn't stop. We asked radio dispatch to run the car registration and to confirm the arrest warrant. We advised them we were following the subject with lights and siren and he was refusing to stop. We followed the poacher to his residence. We contacted him in his driveway, and I advised him he was under arrest for the warrant in Okanogan County.

His wife came to the door when she heard the siren and took the small boy in the house. I advised her that her husband was under arrest and would be taken to jail in Seattle to post bail. I put handcuffs on the poacher, and he sat on the ground next to the front wheel of my buddy's car while we waited on a deputy sheriff to take him to jail. The poacher said his back hurt and he wanted to stand up and sit on the fender of the patrol car.

We stood him up, and he leaned on the fender. After a short time, he jumped up on the hood of the car and started kicking with his heels and put two big dents in the hood and fender of the car. We pulled him off the car, and my buddy wrote him a ticket for destruction of state property. The deputy arrived and transported him to jail. Somehow, he only posted bail for the destruction of property ticket in King County and was released.

He never came to court in Okanogan County, and the warrant was still valid. Several years later, he was arrested again in Olympia for the Okanogan warrant and booked into jail. He was let out of jail to testify for a fire marshal's insurance trial and never posted the bail for the poaching warrant. He never returned to jail or posted the bail and later moved out of state to Alaska! The warrant was still valid.

There were a lot of deer in Okanogan County, and there was always a lot of deer poaching in the northern part of our region. Dale received a report of a man that had killed a deer during the closed season and was living in a cabin at the end of a dead-end road. We had to walk the last half mile as snow had closed the road for the winter. We contacted the man and only found one hindquarter of the deer meat left. He was booked into jail and was found guilty and served a thirty-day jail sentence.

In July of 1986, the USFW service put on a week-long undercover training class for their agents and invited all the state fish and wildlife agencies to let some of their officers attend and receive the training too. All the state had to do was pay for meals and transportation to the Glynco Training Center in Georgia. The fisheries department was going to send three officers, but the game department didn't want to send anybody.

I asked if I could go and pay my own way. I would use my vacation time so it wouldn't cost the state a dime. They finally agreed to let me go, and I learned a lot about investigating wildlife crimes from the training. A very important item was brought up again: Write it down. If you don't write it down today, tomorrow it will be hard to remember what was said. Next month, it will be hard to remember all the facts; and next year will be the same as if the event didn't happen.

When I got back, the chief wanted to know what I thought about starting an undercover unit in the game department. I wrote a report about the training I received and said they couldn't just give the officer an old state truck and $100 buy money and expect to make a lot of arrests. They needed to have an office to work out of, a budget, undercover vehicles and identification, and policies and program direction. I never heard anything more about starting a unit, and nothing happened.

Dale received another deer-poaching report, and we went to contact a suspect. We were in a real mountainous remote area and didn't have radio communications. We tried to sign out at the residence but didn't receive confirmation of our signal. We contacted a man, his wife, and a small child living in a log cabin way back in the timber. We saw rifles sitting in the cabin but didn't find any evidence of deer being killed there.

We took the name and DOB of the man and left. We drove to a

mountaintop and called radio dispatch for a warrant check on the subject. We received an alert tone, and the radio operator came back with an arrest warrant for murder. Dale asked, "What are we going to do?"

I said, "Let's go back and get him."

Dale said, "He has guns in the cabin."

I said, "He won't know we are coming back to arrest him. He will just think we forgot something."

I was driving, and I told Dale I would go up to the door with my portable and he should just step out behind the passenger car door and provide me with backup. I got out and walked up to the door of the cabin, and the man came out just as I got there. He was unarmed, and I advised him he was under arrest for the murder warrant in King County.

I placed him up against the cabin and searched him. He said, "I thought I took care of that." I asked, "Did you have a trial?" He said no.

I asked, "Then what made you think you took care of it?" I cuffed him and took him to the car. His wife came out, and I advised her that we would be taking her husband to the Okanogan jail and he would be transported over to Seattle later to stand trial for the murder warrant.

On the way to jail, our prisoner said that a couple of years ago, two men came to his door in Seattle, and he shot one of them in the face and killed him. As we drove to the jail, he kept gritting his teeth and making growling noises. I asked him if he was okay. He said he was in constant pain and didn't have his medicine. I replied, "Well, your wife can bring it to you before you go over to Seattle." It always amazes me why people move and try to hide and not take care of court orders and think its okay!

The department hired some more wildlife agents, and I was asked to go to Spokane to teach the game code, search and seizure and arrest authority, and firearm training to the new cadets. The Colville tribe sent their law enforcement officers to the class and wanted the department to cross-deputize them to enforce our wildlife laws. They were never commissioned to enforce our laws.

Omak had a community college, and I asked the personnel department if I could have the officers in my detachment take a Spanish class as we worked with and arrested a lot of Hispanic migrant orchard workers. They paid for the four-hour, one night a week, seven-week class. We learned conversational Spanish and the basic questions to ask to gather information for filling out citations and for questioning suspects about killing and possessing deer or other wildlife crimes. It was very helpful.

During the early spring, the department put out new fishing rules, and somebody wanted to change the possession limit of trout from eight to sixteen. I wrote a letter to the director and made a copy for the regional supervisor and my supervisor with my thoughts on the idea. I explained that the local fish biologist and the hatchery manager were doing an excellent job of keeping the local lakes stocked, providing quality trout fishing.

The fishermen could catch a limit in two hours on opening day and have excellent fishing for another two months. If the department doubled the possession limit, the fishing would be over in two weeks. I also said something to the effect of if the administration didn't have anything better to do then sit behind a desk and make life more miserable for the field personnel, they should come over and help me work a check station on opening day. The regional supervisor said, "Those are pretty strong words," but sent the letter on to Olympia.

Over the years, other wildlife agents would complain about the service ammunition the department provided for us to use in our service revolver, saying it wouldn't even kill a raccoon. It was Winchester .38 special (+P) standard police ammo. I shot raccoons, porcupine, and lots of deer with it without any problems.

If I saw a junk car striped and burned in a dump, I would shoot at the doors or trunk, and the bullets would get good penetration. I told the officers they just needed to improve their shooting skills and hit the target in the right spot and the ammo would perform perfectly.

The police and firemen Olympics were being held in Central Washington that year in another month. The liquor control officer was bragging to the border patrol that he and I could beat them in a pistol match. My buddy let his mouth overload his rear end, and they accepted the challenge and beat us. I had the best score, but they outshot my buddy and his big mouth.

We had to buy them milkshakes because my buddy shot so bad he couldn't hit the target. I don't like to lose and was a little upset when I got home. The custom grips of my revolver were a little loose, so I started working on them, wanting a better fit on the frame. I unloaded my revolver and put the cartridges up on the counter and took my revolver in the utility room. I worked on the grips for about an hour, and they fit better.

Some officers shoot holes in doors, mirrors, and TVs practicing quick draw with a loaded firearm. I am a firearms instructor, and preach gun safety all the time to the officers. I tell them to keep the ammo out of the firearm when cleaning or practicing with it. Put the ammo on a table, shelf, or someplace away from the firearm until done practicing. Then change the mind-set and load the firearm and holster it and put it away.

After working on the grips, I loaded my revolver and holstered it. The grips still didn't feel right, so I unloaded it again and put the ammo back up on the counter. I worked on the grips for another half hour and put them back on the revolver, and with the weapon unloaded, dry-fired it for about five minutes. It felt better, so I loaded it once again and holstered it.

As I holstered it, the grips still didn't feel as good as they did a minute ago. I lived alone out in the country, and no one was in the house but me. So I just took my revolver out of the holster and looked at it once more in front of me. With the muzzle pointed in a safe direction, I slowly squeezed the trigger. No mind-set here! At the point of no return, it dawned on me that the revolver was loaded. It went off with a loud bang, and I remember thinking, Damn, that's loud.

I was standing by my back door, so I stepped out onto the deck and looked around to see if anyone was standing close enough to hear the shot. As if that would matter or make it any better. I went back into the entry way and looked at the small round hole in the Sheetrock about a foot above an electrical outlet. I wondered if I had hit the electric wire and ruined the outlet.

I said, "Damn, my refrigerator's on the other side of that wall." The bullet went through the other side of the Sheetrock and entered the back of the refrigerator. I went around to the front of it and opened the door. The bullet went through the back wall and entered the refrigerator, skipped across a Tupperware bowl, punched a hole in a can of grape soda, and came to rest inside the liner of the door without denting the outside.

I guess I could report that bullet still gets good penetration! The bullet missed the electric wire, and I patched the hole in the Sheetrock and bought a can of white spray foam and plugged the hole in the back wall of the refrigerator. I put some freezer tape on the holes in the back and on the hole in the door. It looked like tape that was left on at the factory. My refrigerator still worked fine, but I was very embarrassed and glad I wasn't injured. I learned a very good lesson. I never told anyone about the accidental discharge until after I retired.

I had sold my target pistol, so I borrowed a target pistol from my border patrol buddy and shot in the combat matches at the police and fireman Olympics in Ellensburg in June and won first place and the gold medal. My regional supervisor called me on the radio and wanted to talk to me, so I drove past the office on my way home. I wore my gold medal around my neck when I went into his office.

He asked if I knew what he wanted to talk to me about. I replied, "Well, I just won a gold medal. I thought maybe you wanted to congratulate me." He replied, "No, that ain't it." The director or someone in Olympia hadn't liked what I wrote in my letter about the fish possession limits and wanted to punish me.

My supervisor said it was partly his fault as he shouldn't have sent the letter on to Olympia. I had to take three days of letter writing training in Seattle for punishment. They paid for it, and I got to go see my family and friends in the evenings. Throw me in that brier patch. I'd take all the training they wanted to give me.

I didn't have elk in my patrol district, so after the deer season was over, I was able to hunt elk with my friends during the western rifle season and was able to put a lot of meat in my freezer to eat. I was also able to work in a mule deer hunt in Canada and a mountain goat hunt in Alaska. I bought a fourteen-foot raft and was able to float a lot of white-water rivers with class 5 rapids in Canada, Idaho, Oregon, and Washington.

The game department's name changed to the department of wildlife, and we got a new director and chief of enforcement. The wildlife control division was transferred back over to the enforcement division. All the wildlife agents and control agents had to complete forty hours of training at the Criminal Justice Training Center in Seattle and take a test to give us full police powers in November of 1987. We didn't get a pay raise, just more work.

Over the years, I was fortunate to have been able to use boats, vehicles, snowmobiles, airplanes, horses, and a lot of boot leather making arrests. Hiking into the high lakes to check fishermen was very beautiful, peaceful, and quiet.

SPECIAL INVESTIGATION UNIT

In the summer of 1988, the chief said he was going to start a special investigation unit (SIU) and asked me if I wanted to work undercover with three other officers. I wouldn't get any pay increase but would retain my sergeant's pay grade. I said yes and moved back over to Seattle. We reported directly to the chief, but the department made the mistake that I warned them about several years earlier. They gave us an old state truck and $100 and wanted us to work out of the region office where all the poachers could come to the front desk and see us on any given day, which would blow our cover and ruin an investigation.

I was pretty clean-cut, and a lot of people saw me attend club meetings and would recognize me from all the times my picture was in the newspaper. They suggested I grow a beard and let my hair get longer. We could work in plain clothes but had to wear a sport coat and dress pants when contacting the prosecutor and while attending meetings. We would work on interstate poaching reports and commercial selling of big game and major big game violations turned in by other officers.

Needing a vehicle to drive back and forth to work and for doing routine surveillance, they bought me a blue four-door Oldsmobile sedan with undercover plates. They hid a state radio in the trunk of the car for us to communicate with officers in the field. The car had a car cell phone to call violators and suspects. We were given pagers and voice mail. We were pretty easy to keep track of; however, we only had one computer for the four of us to write reports. They did provide computer training and sent us to the state patrol investigation school.

Changing appearance for working undercover

I bought $15 worth of spray primer paint and was taping off the hood and window of the old gray state truck to paint it in the office warehouse. The regional agent came and asked what I was doing. I told him I was trying to make the truck look like a beater, not a game warden truck. He said, "You can't do that. That's a state truck."

I said, "That's right, and I need to adapt it to my kind of work." I painted the driver's door and the left front fender black and the tailgate a primer brown.

I put some "No Smoking" decals over the holes in the dash where the radio came out of. I put some gray duct tape on the antenna hole on the roof so it wouldn't leak. The USFW gave us some large chrome wheel rims with wide tires. We put an old canopy on the back, and that could keep things dry. It had over 150,000 miles on it, but it ran okay and looked like a Junker.

The other investigators took the decals off their old patrol vehicles and put undercover plates on them for their vehicles. We didn't get paid any more than the other officers, but we could run around without a uniform. Pretty soon a riff started to brew. When they would ask what we were working on, one investigator would say, "I can't tell you, or I will have to kill you" in a joking way. But it caused a lot of friction.

An officer turned in a report of a man selling deer in his district. We bought a blacktail deer fawn from the suspect for $50 and let the officer write the ticket and get the arrest. That smoothed things over a bit. The regional supervisor wanted to use our office space for his staff and wanted to build office space for our unit back in the warehouse.

The department of fisheries started an investigation unit with three officers the same time we started our unit. They didn't have office space either. We pooled our money and rented six small rooms above the net loft from the National Marine Fisheries Service. Bill and Barry shared a room for their office, Deb and I shared a room for our office, and we had a room for evidence.

Fisheries used the other three rooms for their offices. We went to state surplus and picked up used desks and file cabinets and a small table. We were starting to look and be a little more professional and established a case report number system. We still stored frozen evidence in the region's freezer.

Another officer arrested a man for elk poaching and found a ledger book with dates of other wildlife kills. Our unit spent about six months interviewing witnesses and trying to find out if the suspect was selling the elk meat in local restaurants. A lot of bald eagles were documented as killed, and the USFW agents worked with us. The suspect was found guilty and sentenced to three years in jail for killing the eagles.

An officer in Eastern Washington had a hound hunter who had killed two cougars during the closed season and was offering them for sale. He wanted me to come over with some hounds and hook up with the suspect to find out where the cougars pelts were. I told the officer I wasn't going to sleep in the back of a truck with hound dogs and be responsible for them if they ran away. I would come over and pretend I lost my dogs and see if I could contact the suspect.

Another investigator, Barry, and I drove the old gray truck over and stopped at a little grocery store near the suspect's house. I asked the clerk if anyone found any hounds last week and said, "I lost two while hunting bear." She said, "Why don't you ask Ronnie [I'll call him that]? He lives just up the hill." I told her I would look for my dogs that afternoon and contact Ronnie later that evening.

Barry and I drove around and ate dinner and went to Ronnie's house just before dark. Ronnie met us as we stepped out of our truck. He asked, "You the guys looking for some dogs? The gal at the store said you lost a couple." I said, "Yes." He invited us in, and I gave him my song and dance about losing my dogs last week.

I said I had bought a couple dogs from a man in Oregon for $2,000 and was over hunting bear last week and lost them. On the way home, the transmission went out on my other truck. I wanted to hunt cougar this fall, and with all the money I spent already, I would be better off buying one instead of hunting all winter. He took the bait hook, line, and sinker.

In undercover work, we can lie and provide a suspect with an opportunity to commit a violation, but we cannot ask them to commit a violation and then arrest them for it. Ronnie said, "I'll sell you one."

I asked, "What kind?"

He said, "Come on, I'll show you," and took us out to his freezer and showed us the two cougar pelts. I asked, "Where did you get those?"

He said, "They got into my chicken coop last month, and I shot them."

I asked him how much he wanted for one. He said $100. I said, "That sounds like a good deal." I couldn't believe he showed them to us after only knowing us for ten minutes. He asked where I lost the dogs, and I said, "Up on the hill."

He said, "You should go back up there and spend the night, and maybe the dogs will come back. A lot of times they come back to the place where a hunter lets them out of the truck, and the hunter can go back there and pick them back up later."

I told him we would go and spend the night and come back in the morning and buy one of the cougar pelts for $100. We left, and I told Barry, "Now aren't you glad you threw in your sleeping bag and pad?" There wasn't any motels close by, so we were prepared to spend the night in the back of the truck. We parked in the national forest and slept in the back of the truck.

At daylight, I heard a vehicle driving up the road. It was Ronnie. He had his dogs in his truck, and he drove past our location and went on down the road. I told Barry he was checking on us. After a half hour, we drove in the same direction Ronnie had gone. We found Ronnie with a couple of his dogs running around an apple tree.

We pulled up behind him and got out. I told him I didn't find the dogs. Ronnie said, "Well, there is a man who lives over the hill who shoots hounds." Ronnie asked what color my dogs were. I said, "Black and tan."

Ronnie said, "I think I saw them running over in that direction." Ronnie then asked "What are their names?"

What a stupid question; it caught me off guard!

I am generally pretty quick-witted, but I was speechless and couldn't think of a dog's name that sounded appropriate. I looked at Barry, and he just stood there looking at the apple tree. Ronnie was looking at me and wanted an answer, so I said, "Spot." I said one of them had a white spot on his chest, just like the dog Ronnie was holding. He looked at the dog and gave me the old eagle eye of disbelief. I said, "I wonder if that guy stole those dogs. He never did give me any names with 'em."

Ronnie asked, "What was his name?"

I said, "George Smith."

Ronnie said, "I think I know that SOB. I bet he did steal them." I wanted to change the subject and asked where the man lived that shot the hounds and said he better not shoot my dogs. About that time, Ronnie realized his two dogs were loose and starting to drift away from the truck. He said, "I better catch my dogs."

I said, "We will meet you back at your house in an hour and pay you for that cat."

He said, "Okay."

We were driving back to Ronnie's house, and Barry said, "You should have told him you been calling them sons a bit—hes for the last two weeks."

I said, "Well, why didn't you say that an hour ago? You kinda left me hanging out there all alone."

We arrived at Ronnie's house, and he was already there. I paid for the one pelt, and Barry asked if the other pelt was for sale. Ronnie said, "Yes, I want $100 for it too." Barry bought it, and we left.

We made our report, and the local officer had the prosecutor file two counts of sale of illegal wildlife. Ronnie was found guilty in court and fined $400. We all had a good laugh over my invisible dog named Spot. I couldn't believe Ronnie went along with the line of BS I had been putting out.

A Montana game warden working undercover contacted an individual—I will call him Chang—who was buying hard elk antlers in Montana. Chang was also soliciting to buy bear gall bladder. It was illegal to buy or sell bear gall bladder in both Montana and Washington. Chang lived south of Seattle and had an export antler business. The Montana officer made an appointment to meet Chang to sell him a couple bear gall and called me to provide backup and take a video of the transaction for evidence for prosecution.

Most prosecutors require at least three transactions to show an intentional effort to violate before they file charges. That way, it is hard for the defendant to claim we forced him to commit the violation. The Montana officer gave my name to Chang to provide an introduction for me to continue the investigation.

I contacted Chang a week later at the business and introduced myself to him and another partner, whom I will call Sook. I advised them my buddy from Montana said they were interested in buying bear gall bladder. I told them it was illegal to sell or buy bear gall in Washington but I hunted bear and could get some.

They said they knew it was illegal but wanted to buy two from me for $100 each. They didn't know me well enough to trust me and wanted me to bring in the whole bear, not gutted, so they could see the gall bladder come out of the bear. That way, I wouldn't sell them pig gall bladders instead of the real thing. I said if I have to bring in the whole bear, it would cost them $200 each. Chang said okay.

I put out a voice mail to all the wildlife agents and requested two whole dead bears from a damage kill permit or a road kill. I told them to put the bears in a hatchery cooler so it wouldn't spoil and call me. I would come and pick them up. The next week, I received two calls on the same day advising me of two dead bears. After I picked up the dead bears, I called Chang and said I killed two bears and would bring them over the next day. He said okay.

I took pictures of me and the bear and would change clothes several times to make it look like I was a good hunter or poacher and killed a lot of bear. I would lay the photo on the truck dash and show it to the buyers to gain their confidence.

Photo of road killed bear for undercover sales

Barry parked an old van in the parking lot next to the antler business before the business opened to video the transaction for court evidence. I arrived and parked my truck so Barry could see the bears and video the money exchange and went inside to meet Chang. Sook and his wife and his in-laws were the only ones there. Chang could not attend the meeting.

We all went out to look at the bears in the back of my truck, but Sook didn't want to buy the bears in the open in front of the busy street and wanted me to drive around to the back of the warehouse and pull my truck into the warehouse. Barry was afraid something was going to happen to me when he saw me drive into the warehouse.

I unloaded the bears and was going to leave, but Sook wanted me to cut the bears open as he didn't have a knife and he didn't want the carcasses. I told Sook I had the bears lying by a creek to keep them cool but they had bloated a little. When I cut the belly open to pull out and retrieve the liver and gall bladder, I poked the large intestine, and the smelly odor came out.

The women were holding their noses and laughing. I cut the gall bladders off the livers, and Sook paid me $400. He said that now they trusted me and he wanted some more. I said, "I'll call you when I get them." He said, "Okay," and I left and disposed of the two bear carcasses.

After I sold Sook two more bear gall bladders, he wanted to buy some soft velvet antler. I told him that was illegal too, he said, "I know." I gave them my undercover business card with my telephone number, and Sook's wife read it and said, "Oh, you sell wallpaper. We need some for our new house."

I replied, "I only do commercial jobs." Sook patted me on the back and said, "I envy you, Bud. You never work and hunt all the time."

I replied, "Yeah, but you make more money."

I prepared search warrant affidavits and obtained search warrants for the business and Sook's house to serve after the next sale. I sold Sook more gall bladders and velvet deer antler, and then uniformed officers and two more investigators arrived to conduct the searches. When I interviewed Sook, he said, "Why you do this to me, Bud?"

I said, "I told you it was illegal, and you said you knew and did it anyway."

Sook said, "What can I say?"

The office computer and files were seized from the business. More information was obtained about wildlife transactions in Utah. Tax violation information was turned over to the IRS. Chang was fined $4,500 for the purchase of the Montana gall bladders, and Sook was fined $4,500 for the purchase of bear gall and velvet antler in Washington.

A commercial fisherman was arrested for netting steelhead during the closed season. He was found guilty, and the state was going to revoke his commercial license. He said he knew a lot of illegal fishermen and fish buyers and would help the state catch and arrest them if they wouldn't revoke his license.

Our unit met with USFW since some of the fish would be coming from Oregon, and set up a fish-buying company. The USFW said the federal prosecutor didn't want to arrest or target tribal fishermen. We said we would purchase fish product from the tribal members but target the fish companies. Tribal violators would be turned over to the tribe for prosecution.

One of our investigators, Bill, would work with the informant—I will call him Jim—and help us identify some of his poaching associates. Bill and Jim purchased some illegal sturgeon from the Columbia River and sold the meat to one fish company and the eggs to another company. We advised the fisheries department that sturgeon were being caught and sold on the Columbia River.

They didn't believe us and didn't want to work with us on the investigation. Another investigator, Barry, and I would video the transactions and do surveillance and be backup. Sometimes I would go with Jim and sell or buy illegal fish to introduce me as a business partner. Then Bill and I would buy or sell the illegal fish and eggs by ourselves.

Jim and I were going to meet an illegal tribal fisherman—I will call him Madman—and buy closed-season chinook caught from the Columbia River. Madman was complaining about only getting fifty cents a pound for the illegal chinook. I said, "Hey, these fish are illegal. If we get caught with them, we are going to jail. If you got a better offer, take it."

He said, "You white sons ah bitches."

We took the illegal chinook to one of the companies that bought our other illegal fish, and they processed them for us and stored them until the season reopened and we could sell them. I had to sign a receipt, and the company foreman said, "Put your John Henry on this." I said, "You want me to sign it John Henry or John Hancock?"

He knew me as Bud. He said, "Bud ain't a real name. What the hell is your name anyway?" I thought he was suspicious of me and was testing me. I said, "Hey, my momma was a Southern gal, and she named me Buddy Joe. You got a problem with that?"

He said, "Oh no," and never mentioned it again.

I mounted a video camera behind the seat of the old gray truck so we could video the illegal buy or sale of fish produce and the exchange of the money for court evidence. Bill and I bought some illegal steelhead and took the eggs to another egg company on a Sunday to sell to the owner.

We were sitting in the office making small talk, and I asked the owner if he had bought a lot of eggs today. He said, "Hell, the season is closed except for outlaws like you." We all laughed, and he paid us. I bought $1,000 worth of illegal fish from a tribal fisherman that he caught in an hour of fishing. He was turned over to the tribe for prosecution after the investigation was over, and he only received a $25 fine. Where is the justice?

After buying more illegal sturgeon and the female investigator in our unit quitting, we advised fisheries again with evidence of our investigation. It created a rift in our departments, but they provided some officers to assist with compiling the evidence. This investigation took over two years for just the field work. We had over fifty officers assist with serving the search warrants and the searching of eight businesses and homes at the same time and arresting suspects and seizing evidence.

We had documented over one hundred violations of state, federal, and tribal laws. One individual even sold me a stolen outboard motor, and we turned it over to the state patrol. Our SIU had good records, reports, and chain of evidence and received convictions on all the nontribal people and companies we arrested. We received good coverage in all the newspapers.

In 1992, we got another new director and enforcement chief, and there was a rumor going around that a supervisor was going to be appointed for our SIU. The fisheries department was paying their SIU supervisor at a sergeant's pay grade to supervise three investigators.

I wouldn't like working for some of the people whose names were floating around. My name was on top of the inactive sergeant list in the personnel office, so I called the personnel office and put my name back on the active list. If a person's name was on a promotion list and a promotion was offered and it was turned down, the person's name would be taken off the list. If a name was on the inactive list, it was by-passed but not removed and the person could consider a promotion later.

One afternoon, when I was going home, the personnel officer called me and asked if my name was on the active list. I replied, "Yes, I put it back on a month ago." He said, "Okay," and hung up. A short time later, the chief called and said he was going to make a supervisor for SIU. I had a good working relationship with all the field officers, and he wanted me to be the supervisor. He said, "Come down tomorrow morning, and we will get the paperwork done."

I arrived in the Olympia office the next morning in my suit and tie, and the assistant chief said, "We are going to make a supervisor for SIU."

I replied, "I know. That's why I am here." He never liked me that well and said "What?" and gave me a surprised look and jumped up from his chair and went into the chief's office.

Before they closed the door, I heard him say, "How come you didn't tell me about that?" I was promoted back to sergeant and started attending the captain and sergeants' meetings to get a better working relationship between SIU and the rest of the enforcement division.

The fisheries SIU moved their sergeant's office to Olympia, and their two investigators worked out of an office north of Seattle with Bill and Barry. Deb's vacant position was filled with another investigator named Bill, and I found another office and warehouse for our equipment south of Tacoma, closer to Olympia. Two more investigators were assigned to the Columbia River, one for fisheries and one for wildlife.

Our department purchased a twenty-three-foot motor home with some federal money to monitor the endangered fish on the Columbia River. It was on my inventory, and I was responsible for taking care of it and keeping it clean. On the maiden voyage after buying groceries for the trip, I started driving to the campground to do some surveillance work. Halfway there, the refrigerator door came open, and a plastic gallon jug of milk fell out onto the floor and the lid came off. What a mess!

The milk spilled all over the floor and ran up and down the hallway until I could find a wide spot beside the highway to pull over and stop. The milk also ran under the cabinets. I put an external lock on the refrigerator door and had to clean the RV twice to get the soured milk smell out of it. I held a training class with the other investigators on driving and operating it. It had curtains on the windows, so we could park on a boat launch and monitor and document any violations and radio a field officer to contact the violator for an arrest.

An officer wanted SIU to monitor the silver salmon catch at Neah Bay and investigate an unlicensed fishing guide. The motels in that area were pretty dumpy; I drove the motor home over and parked in the campground with all the other fishermen. That way, the other investigators could document fishermen cleaning salmon and going back for over limits.

I put a neck brace around my neck and would sit on the dock and watch for violations. I observed the suspect—I will call him John—coming in from a fishing trip. I walked past his boat as he was unloading his catch. We started talking, and I gave him my song and dance about someone wrecking my boat and how I hadn't had a chance to get out on the water to fish that morning. John said, "I'll take you," and gave me a business card and said, "Call me Monday night. I can take you next weekend."

I called John and set up a trip for the next weekend. John said, "I don't fish like the other people. I put down my lines and just hog the fish in so we can catch our limits and go back out for another limit later."

I said, "Well, whatever works for you," and agreed on a price for Bill, Barry, and myself. I contacted the local officer and told him to watch for our return to the dock and witness the money exchange and come down and arrest the suspect.

I would help John with lowering the downriggers and hooking up the fishing lines. John said, "You must have done that before," and complimented me for doing a good job. We fished for four hours and returned to the dock. The fishing wasn't too good, and we only caught a couple silver salmon.

After paying John with marked bills, I said, "Maybe we'll try again another day," and left. The local officer contacted John and arrested him and confiscated the money. When the officer was issuing the citation, he asked John about us. John said he never knew us before that day but that the Bud guy was a really nice guy. I told you, even poachers liked me.

Alaska Fish and Game contacted me and wanted an investigation started on a subject, whom I will call Gary, living in Washington and guiding bear hunters in Alaska without a guide's license. Alaska would pay my expenses if I could line up a bear hunt. The Northwestern States, Alaska, and Canadian wildlife agencies had a memorandum of understanding between one another to cooperate on joint state violators.

Gary worked in an archery shop south of Tacoma. I contacted Gary at the shop and bought a dozen arrows. We went to a coffee shop for lunch, and Gary offered me a guided Alaska bear hunt to start a couple months later. I contacted the Alaska SIU, and the supervisor sent a check for plane fare and the bear hunt fee. I went to the archery shop and paid

Gary the down payment for the hunt and shot in an archery target competition.

I flew to Alaska and met with Alaska SIU investigators who would make the arrest. They advised that Gary was not licensed to guide hunters and didn't have any licensed bait stations. Later that night, I met three other hunters, as prearranged by Gary, and we took a ferry to the Prince of Wales Island to meet Gary. After riding in the back of an open pickup on a pile of firewood blocks, I could see right away this was not going to be a first-class guided hunt.

The camp was a fourteen-by-sixteen-foot canvas tent set up beside a big puddle of water. Everybody would wash their muddy boots off and pee in the puddle of water. Six canvas cots were lined side by side, six inches apart, on one side of the tent. A wood stove and card table were on the other side, and a box of food sat on the mud floor. A dirty pot of cheese macaroni left over from lunch was sitting on the stove.

Gary went out and washed the pot in the puddle of water next to the tent and came in and asked if anybody wanted any dinner. He would fix some. I said no, I wasn't hungry. I don't remember what Gary fixed for the rest of the hunters. Breakfast was dry cereal and milk and a stale donut. At least the paper bowl was clean. I could eat out of it. We stopped in a small town, after scouting for bear, and I called the ASIU office to give the officers our camp location. I bought a sandwich, bottled water, and all the junk food I could fit in my pockets.

I sat on bear bait that afternoon without seeing any bear. Two others hunters stayed out all night, and one killed two black bears: a sow and a cub. We hunted the next morning without seeing any bear. One of the other hunters started complaining about the camp conditions and the hunting and wanted to leave.

I was supposed to meet the ASIU investigators that evening in another town, so it made it easy for me to complain and want to leave too. I took a floatplane back to town and was going to meet the ASIU investigators. The other hunter got on the same floatplane and wanted to accompany me back to Seattle.

Arriving at the airport, I told the other hunter that I had an old girlfriend in Anchorage and wanted to see her. I went to a telephone and stood by it for ten minutes, pretending to talk to her. I went back and told the other hunter I was going to fly to Anchorage to meet her and wouldn't be flying back to Seattle with him. He said, "Have fun," and boarded the plane to Seattle.

After spending the night discussing the case facts with ASIU investigators, we prepared to meet with the local fish and game officer the next day. The Alaska officers contacted Gary and arrested him for guiding without a license and operating unlicensed bear bait stations. The other hunter was charged with killing over the daily limit of bear. All the defendants pleaded guilty or forfeited bail, and I didn't have to go back to testify in court.

I started an investigation into the illegal trafficking of bear gall in Washington. Bill would work with me and would video or assist in selling bear galls to six different markets. I arrived at a market and parked so Bill could video the transaction. The suspect wanted me to park on the other side of the building so a group of loggers couldn't see us. I moved the truck and started my video camera in my truck, and a drunk came staggering up.

He was wanting in my truck, and I told him, "Get the hell out of here." I locked the truck door behind me and went into the store and sold the bear gall and bear paws. When I went back out to the truck, I realized I had locked the keys in the ignition. I had to go back into the store and get a coat hanger to unlock my truck. It only took me about three minutes to get in, and the suspect said, "Boy, you're pretty good at that." Bill was sitting across the street wondering what I was doing.

After making three sales to each of the markets, we contacted the local officers, and they contacted the markets and arrested the suspects and questioned them about Bill and me. Bill was shorter than me and had black hair and a beard. I was tall with gray hair and a beard. We are as different as day and night. The Asian woman suspect told the officer, "You know those white guys, they all look alike." We had another good laugh.

I was able to go white-water rafting on the Bio Bio River in Chile before the Chilean Government dammed it for hydroelectric power. I found it a poor country, still using oxen and wooden carts for farming. I really missed drinking milk.

Catching fish for breakfast on the Bio Bio River in Chile

An officer (Chuck) in Yakima wanted me to help investigate an elk poacher. The suspect, whom I will call Clem, lived over on the west side of the mountains near me. I ran a background check and obtained his driver's license picture and told Chuck that Clem might know me as working for the wildlife department. Chuck wanted me to come over and contact Clem with him.

Chuck and I drove into Clem's camp, and Clem met us at the gate. He looked at Chuck and said, "Is this your game warden buddy?" I replied, "Yeah, how much do they make? I wouldn't mind having a badge."

Clem said "I've got something for you," and turned back toward his motor home. Chuck said, "He's going for a gun. Let's keep close to him." We were unarmed and stood outside the door on high alert with mixed feelings.

Clem came out with a package of smoked pork and no gun. We sat around camp, and Chuck and Clem had a beer. Clem started accusing Chuck of turning him in to the game wardens and said they had come and searched his house over the weekend. Chuck said, "I didn't turn you in to anybody."

Clem said, "Well, you're the only one I told about that mountain goat." We knew nobody searched Clem's house. He must have been testing us.

I recognized Clem as the one who shot with me at Gary's archery shop in Yelm. Clem was probably too drunk to remember me, but he was suspicious of me. So I said, "Chuck, let's get the hell out of here. I came over here to hunt bear. I didn't come over here to be called a game warden."

Clem said, "Ah, sit down. You could be the best undercover game wardens in the world, and you couldn't arrest me because I'm part

Cherokee Indian." Clem settled down and had another beer.

Clem wanted to go spotlighting for elk that evening. He was still drinking, but we agreed to go with him and meet him around 9:30 pm. Clem had a loaded .22 Mag rifle next to him on the front seat of his jeep. Chuck was in the passenger seat, and I sat in the back seat behind Chuck. We rode around for a couple hours and didn't see any elk or deer. Clem was on his sixth beer and almost drove off the left side of the mountain road.

The left front tire was just about off the edge of the hill, and I yelled at Chuck, "Look out!" I opened the back door and stepped out onto the road. I thought they were going over the edge and down the mountain. Chuck grabbed the steering wheel and steered the jeep back onto the road. I don't drink and was sober, so I told Clem, "Let me drive, and you spotlight for a while." We rode around for another half hour and then went back to camp.

I told Clem I was going bear hunting in the morning and wanted to get some sleep. Chuck and I went back to our camp and wrote down notes for out reports. Clem drove by, and we could see him spotlighting another road system. I told Chuck, "Clem is checking to see if we went back to camp." The next morning, Clem's wife was coming to help take down their camp and head home. I told Chuck I couldn't go back to Clem's camp because she would recognize me from having attended the archery shoot and having their friend arrested in Alaska.

The next morning, I walked down the creek and stayed in the timber across from Clem's camp for backup while Chuck stopped by the camp. Clem had already left, and the camp was deserted. We went home, and Chuck introduced Bill to Clem. They continued the investigation for three more months.

Clem was arrested, and I had to testify later about the spotlighting in Yakima County. The jury's eyes lit up when I testified about Clem telling me I could be the best undercover game warden in the world and couldn't arrest him. Clem's attorney was trying to convince the jury that we were all drunk and asked me how I could remember how many beers Clem and Chuck drank that day. I said it was because I didn't drink and was sober and I wrote it down. Clem was found guilty and received three years in jail for the total of all his violations.

It was illegal to sell cougar in Washington, and a suspect put an advertisement in a game breeder's magazine and offered to sell cougar kittens. I called the number, and the suspect, whom I will call Bob, said he wanted $600 for a kitten. Bob told me it was illegal to sell them in Washington, so we would have to go to Idaho or Oregon to make the transfer of money. I made an appointment to meet Bob and his wife and see the cougars the next week. After the call, I wrote out a report on my laptop computer for the investigation file. The timing of that report would be very important years later.

Bob could hold cougars in captivity under a permit, but he could not sell them. Bob had several adult cougars, and one got pregnant and had three kittens: two males and a female, which were three months old. I looked at them and told Bob I would buy the one he called Charlie. I was about to leave, and I asked Bob if he wanted me to give him a $100 for a down payment on the kitten. Bob said that would be good, and I wrote him a check for $100 and left.

That night, Bob called me and was worried about my check. I told him it was good but I would bring $600 in cash next week and then we could go to Oregon to make the transfer. I contacted the local wildlife agent and prosecutor and obtained a search warrant and arranged for a crew of officers to come and search Bob's residence after I paid him the $600 in marked bills and seize the money and other cougar kittens.

I arrived as planned and held Charlie and asked, "How will I know I am getting the same kitten?" Bob picked up a pen and marked a paw on the kitten with a black felt marker. I paid Bob the $600, and they gave me back my $100 check. I left and called the officers to come on in and make the search and advised them about the marked paw on Charlie.

As I drove away, Bob followed me down the driveway, planning to leave too. I didn't want Bob to leave until the officers got there to retrieve the marked money. I stopped at the end of his driveway to ask Bob what I needed to bring next week when I picked up the kitten. The officers pulled up in marked cars, and Bob said, "Get out of here." I left, and the officers stopped and talked to Bob. And then they all went back up to the house to retrieve the money and seized all three kittens.

I contacted the prosecutor, and he charged Bob with selling cougar contrary to Washington game laws. Bob was found guilty in court. He hired an attorney and appealed the case, claiming the cougar was a South American cougar subspecies and not native to North American and that it didn't fall under Washington law. The appeals court reversed the guilty verdict and found Bob not guilty. Bob sued me and the wildlife department for $5,000,000.

I took blood samples, and the crime lab found the cougar kittens were mixed blood with North American cougar and the AG's office appealed the not guilty decision. The case was appealed and reversed again and Bob was found guilty again. Bob appealed, and the case went back and forth with appeals for over eight years. The cougar kittens grew into adults, and I had to find a permanent place to house and hold them for evidence. The Olympic Game Farm agreed to keep and feed them for a monthly fee until the case was final.

The chief wanted me to move my office into the Olympia headquarters, and once again I was sitting at a desk where all the poachers could see me. Bill worked out of the state patrol office with the troopers to make his reports. The Fisheries SIU supervisor's position was upgraded to a captain's pay grade.

Six months later, I petitioned the wildlife personnel office to upgrade my position to a captain. I had to supervise more investigators and work with twice as many field officers and a bigger land area. On October 25, 1993, I was promoted to captain, and my pay was upgraded. I had come a long way from that little one-room Lutheran schoolhouse in rural Illinois.

My promotion was short-lived as Fisheries and Wildlife merged in 1994 and was called the Washington Department of Fish and Wildlife (WDFW). The Fisheries chief was appointed as the chief of enforcement and the chief of Wildlife was appointed assistant chief.

The Fisheries SIU captain had six months more seniority working for the state then I did and was appointed as captain of our now joint SIU unit. I would have to bump the captain in Aberdeen, and he would have to bump the captain in Spokane and start a domino effect all over the state, or I could take an investigator's position and get captain's pay. Ahh, let me think about this for a minute? I get captain's pay and don't have to supervise anybody? Throw me in that briar patch!

The captain of SIU took my old desk and moved me and several other investigators into office space in the warehouse. At least the poachers couldn't see us every day. An officer over by Port Townsend arrested a diver—I will call him George—for illegal possession of abalone. George was found guilty in court, and the state was going to revoke his commercial license. He contacted SIU and wanted to work as a confidential informant (CI).

My captain called a meeting with National Marine Fisheries, USFW, and the investigators to discuss the options. The CI had a bad reputation, and the other agencies didn't want to be involved with the investigation. I had found out over the years that it was an occupational hazard to be single. The married investigators didn't want to work away from home for any extended period of time, and I ended up doing a lot more work and traveling than they did.

My captain wanted me to work with the CI as a deckhand on a twenty-five-foot dive boat four days straight for eight weeks. With a half-day travel on both ends of the work period, that took up six days of the week. They wanted me to sell geoduck clams to illegal divers on the seventh day. My captain didn't want to pay me any overtime or comp time, just eight hours a day. I told him I wouldn't do it without some compensation for working seven days a week for eight weeks straight.

He agreed to pay me comp time for anything over eight hours a day. George was injured in a boat fire accident, and it took a long time getting the investigation started. So I attended a diver's union meeting and met a lot of the suspected poachers. I would camp in the motor home at a campground in Friday Harbor and work all day on the boat. Then George and I would sit in a tavern until 9:00 or 10:00 pm and talk with other poachers and make plans to buy and sell illegal geoducks.

That first week I had to walk a mile, back and forth, to town and the campground until I could drive an undercover truck there to drive the next week. Other investigators would stay in the motel and provide backup onshore that first week. I could call them on a cell phone at night from the motor home to communicate with them about other poachers and violations.

Another poacher diver had a special tank built into the bottom of his boat to hide illegal sea cucumbers. He had a six-inch hole in the floor of his boat to put the sea cucumbers through into the tank. A boat seat fitted on a six-inch pipe plugged the hole in the floor so Fisheries officers couldn't see it. The diver would pull the boat into his shop so no one could see him take the illegal sea cucumbers out of a hole that was below the waterline in the transom.

I advised the local officer, and he caught the poacher with a boat full of illegal sea cucumbers and arrested him, the twenty-five-foot boat was seized for evidence. The poacher was found guilty in court and fined $5,000, and the boat was confiscated.

There were two other divers working on George's boat, and I had to be careful when I wrote my notes for my reports. I would keep a small notebook in my extra pair of shoes in the boat cabin and would make notes when I ate lunch. I would make a more detailed report in the motor home after coming home from the tavern each night.

I wore the same black sweatshirt and blue sweatpants for the whole investigation. I had to put them in a plastic bag so they wouldn't smell up the RV on the weekends. My girlfriend said if any crook had half a brain, they would know I wasn't a bad guy because I took a bath and was too clean.

Another investigator would debrief the CI and make a report of his activities when he was away from me. I would arrive at Friday Harbor on Saturday afternoon and meet George for dinner with the other poachers. I told them I was a reformed alcoholic and didn't drink anymore because I got real mean when I drank. They never questioned me about it and accepted me always drinking 7 Up.

The first night in the tavern, one of the divers on our boat was half drunk and wanted to get into a head-butting contest with another poacher. The last time he did that, he ended up in the hospital with a concussion. I told the poacher's buddy to put a stop to the contest because I had a lot of money invested in George's boat and wanted the diver to make some of it back for me. He couldn't do that from a hospital bed. They finally decided not to head butt.

If that wasn't enough for me to worry about, George was half drunk and started to say he was an undercover game warden. I kicked him real hard under the table before anyone heard him. He asked, "What the hell you doing, kicking me?"

I replied, "Don't ever give them an idea that I might be a game warden." I was a stranger to them, and they didn't trust me anyway.

The season was closed on Sunday, but the dive boats could go out and test areas before it opened. Some boats would put urchins in bags and mark the spot and come back during the open season Monday through Wednesday and pick them up. We would start work at 6:00 am, and I would pull in four-hundred-pound bags of red or green sea urchins until it was dark and then sell them each night to a buyer at the dock. By the time I got back that night and finished writing my notes, it was a fifteen- to sixteen-hour day.

The diver had an oxygen-supplied dry dive suit, and he would collect the urchins and put them in a large mesh bag. Then he would fill a smaller plastic bag with oxygen, and it would lift the urchins to the surface. I would hook a line to the bag and winch it into the bow of the boat. I had to coil and feed out the air hose to the diver when he was underwater. I was fifty-four years old, twice as old as the other deckhands, but I would pull in more urchins than the other boats every day.

We would sell between six to eight thousand pounds a day for sixty-five cents a pound. One day the diver got mad at me and was jerking the air hose and started cursing me on the speaker system that we used to talk on for communications. When he came up after his shift, I got in his face and said, "Don't you ever cuss me again. I didn't do anything to you, and I am feeding out the air hose as fast as I can. If you can't ask me for a little more hose in a nice way, I'll put a kink in your damn air hose and see how long you can stay down without it." He never did that again.

George had a reputation for being a tough guy, and one day, another dive boat anchored within 150 feet of our boat and was going to go down and pick urchins. George cussed him and told him to leave and threatened to shoot a flare gun into his boat. I told him he better not and had to take the flare gun away from him.

One day the diver's union president was riding in our boat, and the water was too rough to go out to test on a closed day. He said, "Bud, you seem like a nice guy. How did you get mixed up with a bunch like this?"

I replied, "Well, I am a shirttail relative of George, and he got hurt. I loaned him some money, so I am just trying to get some of it back."

He said, "Well, watch yourself."

One of the divers George knew wanted to buy some illegal geoducks. There was a geoduck season for divers, but they had to pay the state a $4.50 per pound fee for everything they harvested and could only sell them for $7.50. They only made a $3.00 pound profit after working all day. It was easier to buy geoduck illegally for $5.00 a pound and sell them on the black market for $7.50. They would make a $2.50 profit and be money ahead without having to work all day.

The state shellfish biologist would collect and sample clams and geoduck to see if they were safe to eat before a season was opened. I contacted the biologist and requested three hundred pounds of geoduck for my undercover sale. I had to get up at 3:00 am on my day off from the dive boat and drive to the hatchery and pick them up before other state workers got there. I would arrange for other investigators to video the transaction, then George and I would contact the suspect.

This suspect, whom I will call Dale, was out of jail on work release for another clam-poaching violation and wasn't too smart. Dale told George that he was suspicious the state would try and set him up again and was going to have a shotgun with him and vowed to shoot any fish cop that showed up. I carried a little .380 semiautomatic pistol inside my jacket pocket, and I told George if I stuck my hand in my jacket, he better duck because I was going to start shooting.

Another investigator's undercover van was parked in the parking lot to video the sale, and Dale showed up and was real spooky. He backed up to my truck and didn't want to get out or make the sale there. He wanted to move, but I had the camera running in my truck and I didn't want to move either. I said to Dale, "These garbage cans are heavy. Can't you help pull them into your van?" I looked to see if he had a shotgun and watched Dale when he got up to help.

Other officers were going to follow Dale and find out where he sold them. They lost him for about a half hour but saw him again as he crossed the Tacoma Narrows Bridge and followed him to a parking lot past the suspected market. The next day, when Dale paid me $1,500 cash, he told me what happened. Dale said he saw a man carrying a newspaper under his arm walking in front of the market and thought he might be a cop.

Dale said that spooked him. So he drove to a parking lot and called the owner, and they made the sale there. Dale said the owner paid him in $100 bills, so he took them to a bank and exchanged them into $50 bills. He looked me in the eye and said, "Fisheries ain't sophisticated enough to catch me," as he handed me the money. I wanted to throw him down on the ground and say, "Caught you." It was all I could do to keep from laughing in Dale's face. He was arrested two months later.

Surprise! Game warden. You're under arrest.

Another diver wanted to buy some illegal geoducks too. I had to request another three hundred pounds from the biologist and set up the sale with the suspect. I had another investigator video that sale. The suspect was a little suspicious of me and told me he had a brother in jail and if anybody messed with him, he'd have his brother kill 'em. I said, "Well, a man has to protect his family." The suspect didn't know what to say. He just paid me the $1,500 and left. He was also arrested two months later.

The urchin season closed on December 24, Christmas Eve, and we worked late in the day to get a boatload of urchins. I was running late and had to get the motor home and get back to the ferry dock in a half hour or wait for the next one to run in the morning. I didn't want to work on Christmas Day, so I ran the mile to the campground. The water hose and sewer line were frozen on the motor home, and I had a hard time getting them off and stored away. It was making me later still.

The steps were frozen too, and I kicked them real hard and flipped them up and mashed my right thumbnail. It hurt like heck, but I made it to the ferry. My thumbnail turned black and was hurting so bad I had to go to the emergency room on Christmas Day and have a hole burned into the thumbnail to let the blood out and relieve the pressure. I worked on the dive boat for eight weeks and built up a lot of comp time but ruptured my hernia and had to have it operated on. It's hell to get old and try to work like a twenty-one-year-old.

I worked a lot of undercover investigations by myself without backup and was very lucky nothing happened to me. Sometimes I would carry a Smith & Wesson .44 Mag in a canvas holster. It didn't look like a cop gun, and the poachers weren't too suspicious of me. I was hunting with a group of hound hunters that were reportedly selling bear gall, and their hounds had treed a 150-pound black bear up a fir tree.

I was riding in one of their trucks, and we parked on an abandoned log road. Some people had been peeling cascara bark from all the trees in the area, and it looked like they had camped on the road and went to the bathroom right in the middle of the road. We had to watch where we stepped going to get the bear.

I had the permit to hunt the bear, so they asked me to shoot it. I took aim with the .44 and shot it in the head, and it fell to the ground. Then one poacher yelled, "Shoot it again." I was still pretty good with a pistol and saw the impact of the bullet on the head of the bear and knew it was dead, but I shot again. We dragged the bear back to the truck, and the hounds ran ahead of us. They rolled in the human poop and had it all over their collars.

One hunter caught his dog by the collar and got it all over his hands, and he was vomiting and screaming at the dogs. He had the dry heaves and told his young son to take the collars and wash them off in the creek. Some of the dogs walked in the poop and climbed up on the dog box in the back of the truck and just laid there.

It was lunchtime, and one of the hunters—I will call him Jim— who pulled the bear back to the truck and never washed his hands took a loaf of bread out of his truck. Jim laid two slices of the bread on the dirty dog box and pulled some bologna out of a cooler. Jim laid the bologna on the bread slices with his dirty hands and asked me if I wanted a sandwich. I said, "No, I ate my lunch in the other truck." I still liked to eat clean food!

We took the bear over to the creek by the road bridge, and Jim gutted the bear. He put rocks in the chest cavity to weigh it down and put the bear carcass in the creek water to keep it cool. He threw the guts with the liver and gall bladder up under the bridge so the dogs wouldn't get it. We hunted the rest of the day without treeing another bear. Jim said we should quit and he would go get my bear and take it to my truck for me. I knew he wanted the gall bladder.

I told the group I had an Asian girlfriend and her dad wanted the gall bladder, so I would go with Jim and retrieve it. Jim said the dogs ate it. I said, "No, they didn't. I saw you throw it up under the bridge, and I want to go get it for her dad." It got awfully quiet, and Jim was steaming mad at me for calling him a liar. There were four of them and just little old me!

I didn't know if I was going to have to fight him or if the group was going to dump me out and leave me all alone fifty miles from the nearest town. I knew which way was north but didn't know if this road would come out on the highway. We went back to the bridge, and I got the gall bladder without any trouble. They took me back to my truck. I sold the gall bladder on another investigation.

Canada's SIU supervisor, Bill Bresser, called me and wanted me to work an illegal guide suspect for him. I had worked an illegal fishing guide for Bill several years earlier and had also presented a program about working undercover on wildlife cases to some of the Canadian Mounties. Bill provided me with the telephone number of the licensed guide who was operating illegal bear hunts for US hunters. I called the number and spoke to a man I will call John and told him that a friend told me about his guide service and that I wanted to hunt a spring bear. John said he had over

200,000 acres of hunting territory with his license and had a lot of real big bear. He quoted me a price, and I replied that it sounded fair and set a date to hunt around the end of May. John said to call him when I got to the small town of Hope and he would meet me.

After setting the hunt date, I called Bill and advised him of the hunt, and he instructed me to meet one of his investigators at the border when I came up for the hunt. They would provide me with money for the hunt and a notebook to write down notes for a final report, and they would pick it up after the hunt was over, along with the bear for court evidence.

I would be hunting alone without any back up again, and I couldn't bring my .44 Mag into Canada. At least I would have my rifle with me, and I always carried a compass and a knife. I had white-water rafted the rivers in this area several times and had a little knowledge of the terrain. I met the CSIU investigator after crossing the US border into Canada and received instructions, money, a notebook, and a phone number to call for a meeting place after the hunt.

I would hunt for three days and exchange the notebook and evidence before going back to the US. I called John from Hope, and he met me. I followed him to his residence. John lived in a trailer, and the overall appearance of the place was pretty dumpy. Why couldn't I ever get a first-class outfit for one of these undercover hunts? Maybe because they are illegal?

Several other US hunters from Texas were there and two of Johns guides. John's son-in-law would be guiding me. He was real short, and we looked like an odd couple. John hired a cook, and we ate our meals at his trailer. She fixed good wholesome meals; at least the food was good. We slept in another trailer made into a bunkhouse. When I looked at the truck we would be hunting out of, I thought it needed a few more screws and another piece of baling wire to hold it together.

We saw a bear the first afternoon, but I told the guide it was too small. I didn't shoot it. When we hunted another area, my guide drove the wrong way on the highway exit ramps to get to another hunting area. I wrote down directions and locations where we hunted, and later CSIU located them on maps and found that we hunted in areas that didn't belong to the outfitter.

On the second day of hunting, I saw a bear about a mile away feeding in a logged-off clear-cut. The guide couldn't believe I could see that far and said, "That's a stump."

I said, "No, it's a bear."

We drove to within a half mile of the bear, and the guide said,

"Oh, it's a big one. Get ready to shoot it."

I said, "It looks pretty small to me."

The guide again said, "No, it real big. Load your rifle, and we'll drive closer. Then you step out and shoot it."

We drove to within two hundred yards. I got out, and the guide said, "Shoot it before it gets away."

I replied, "It's a small bear. Let's look for a bigger one."

He said, "No, shoot it." The bear was next to a patch of timber, and when I shot, it ran a short distance and disappeared into the timber. The guide said, "You missed it."

I replied, "No I hit it. It will be dead, just inside the timber."

We had to drive up the road a quarter mile and park by a washout on an abandon road that went to the timber. I carried my rifle, and we looked for blood in the clear-cut. We could see tracks but couldn't see any blood as it was getting dark. I told the guide, "I know I hit it. It should be dead." He didn't have a rifle, so he wanted me to walk in front of him with my rifle. I said "I can smell it. It's lying around here somewhere." Then I saw it lying in a small depression next to a big fir log.

The guide walked over to it, and I replied, "Hell, it's a baby." It was a hundred-pound sow, and the guide said, "You don't have to tag it. We'll leave it here in the timber and hunt again tomorrow for a bigger bear. If we don't find another one, you can tag this one, and take it home." He gutted it and laid it on the big log. It was dark, so we quit for the evening and headed back to the trailer. My guide said, "Don't tell John you killed this one."

We both smelled like bear, and if John was much of a guide, he would know we got one today. Nobody mentioned the bear at supper, and I went to the bunkhouse and made some notes in the bathroom. The next morning, my guide was extra tired, and it looked like he was falling asleep as he was driving. I told him I was tired and asked for him to pull off the highway and take a nap. We pulled over and slept for an hour.

I only had thirty more days to work, and then I would retire. I didn't want to have a record of working thirty-one-and-a-half years chasing poachers and then getting killed in a vehicle crash a month before I retired. We hunted another area with a lot of rough water bars cut across the road to keep them from washing out. Every time we crossed a water bar, the truck would die. The steering wheel had a short in the wiring, and the motor would shut off.

As we were driving home that evening in the dark, the truck would die. The guide would wiggle the steering wheel, and it would start again. The lights kept going out, so he turned them off and drove sixty miles per hour on the highway without lights. I again thought I was going to die before I could retire. We finally made it to the guide's trailer safe!

The guide said his brother-in-law had gone up and skinned the hide off the bear I shot the day before and had it at the trailer. I could tag it tomorrow before I went home. John said I would have to have the bear hide inspected at the border and called to make arrangements to have an inspector there when I crossed on Sunday.

I paid for the hunt and left around noon to meet the CSIU investigator as planned. We exchanged notes and evidence, and I went home. The investigator took the bear hide to his office for evidence, and I never checked it through customs.

The next day, John called me and said, "What you trying to do, get me arrested? You didn't check that bear hide in, and I'll get in trouble." I told John I had gone to Vancouver and met an old girlfriend and given her the bear hide. It was so small I didn't want to bring it back home. He calmed down and said, "Good."

The CSIU continued the investigation for another year with other hunters, and the case never came to court until after I retired. I was subpoenaed into court to testify four years later. John was convicted, and he lost his guide license and his 200,000-acre guide area.

I was only fifty-five and in good health, but the politics and infighting between Wildlife and Fisheries was so bad in the department after the merger that I just wanted to retire and enjoy the rest of my life with my new bride. My supervisor said, "He was working his way up to be chief," and wanted me to be his assistant chief. I told him I didn't want to be his gopher and do all his grunt work.

After working thirty-one-and-a-half years as a wildlife enforcement officer, I retired on June 30, 1996, and moved to Alaska to enjoy and experience the last great frontier. During my career, I was able to attend two North American Wildlife Enforcement Officers Association conventions and exchange ideas and information with many officers from other states.

All the officers were in dress uniform and looked very professional. I had my beard and long hair and wore jeans, a sports jacket, a cowboy hat, and boots. Everyone had to stand and introduce themselves, their name, title, and the state they worked. I stood up and said, "I am an actor. I pretend I don't work for the Washington Wildlife Enforcement Division."

I had a friend from Ohio living in Anchorage who worked for the Federal Fish and Wildlife Service, and I knew and had worked with several of the Alaska Fish and Game investigators. They were always too busy working, so I had to recreate by myself. I met a wildlife biologist and helped him conduct a grouse survey. I still enjoy seeing and working with wildlife.

In 1997, I moved to Montana and built a house and enjoyed hunting and fishing. I met the local fish and wildlife officers and helped them check hunters at a check station. I worked on the federal waterfowl refuge north of town and put up and maintained a wood duck box nest program. I would also fly in a helicopter with the state wildlife biologist and count deer, elk, and bighorn sheep on his annual survey. My wife said, "I thought you retired. You're not getting paid to do that anymore."

Six years after I retired, I was called back to Washington to be deposed by Bob's attorney for the $5,000,000 cougar kitten lawsuit. I testified to the facts in my reports, and Bob's attorney asked, "How can you remember those facts so clearly?"

I replied, "I wrote it down."

He asked, "When?"

I replied, "On the day I made the telephone call."

His attorney asked, "Where does it say that?"

I said, "On the bottom of the paper you have in your hand.

The footnote on my report said the information was collected by Officer Holste on 00/00/00 and the report was completed by me on the same day. Bob's attorney looked at it and said, "Oh." He had the paper in his possession for almost ten years and hadn't read it. The appeals court reversed the case a third time, and Bob moved out of state and dropped the lawsuit eight years after I retired. A very important fact is to write it down now.

A poacher is a thief and steals your opportunity to harvest a trophy or put meat in the freezer. Turn in a poacher, and get a reward or bonus points for a special draw permit. If you find someone poaching, arrest him for me as I like to eat fish and wildlife meat too. If you find a young kid breaking the law and it's not too serious, give the kid a break, and maybe he will end up being the next generation game warden. And that is the way it was in my life as a game warden. The DNA test results for a game protector, a wildlife agent, a sergeant, a special investigator and a captain, all came back to one and the same person, a game warden called Bud. The common gene found in them all, an inquisitive mind.

A midmorning duel in Montana after retiring

ABOUT THE AUTHOR

When Harold "Bud" L. Holste was a child in grade school,
he spent a lot of time watching a fox squirrel eating a walnut outside
the window by his desk. Bud loved watching wildlife and has come
a long way from being one of the two first-graders in 1946 in that
little one-room school in the rural farm community known as Blue
Point, Illinois. Bud was never rich or famous; few people hardly
know his name. He has made mostly good choices in his life as he
grew to maturity.

Bud was very fortunate that he didn't drown as a teenager or
have to jump off a railroad bridge. He was also lucky that he was
never arrested for poaching when he was a young adult. Those things
would have prevented him from being a game warden in Ohio and
Washington. Bud is retired now but still has dreams of working and
arresting poachers. The poachers say, "You can't arrest me, you're
retired." Bud tells them, "My commission is still good for three more
days." Bud never went crazy, and at least he is now dreaming in the
retirement mode and not about getting shot.

Working on the farm for fifty cents a day when he was a
young boy and pouring concrete in the hot sun when it was ninety-
six degrees out after high school helped Bud make up his mind to
choose a different career path. It seemed like he was always going
uphill for most of his career, but Bud enjoyed a challenge and was

proud to be called a game warden.

He is very thankful to have succeeded and promoted to the rank of captain without having a college education. Most promotions, however, seemed to come at an inappropriate time when he couldn't afford to move or had just bought a new house.

Be very mindful of the weather and people around you and always expect the unexpected. Be ready to react to the ever-changing conditions. Bud was always very quiet when he was walking up to a poacher. It made him feel good when he could walk up to them in full uniform and arrest them when they were violating some law. Bud also enjoyed catching the hardened criminals and tricking them when working undercover too. Bud would want to thank all the concerned citizens and sportsmen and women who reported wildlife violations and turned in a relative or friend to help protect wildlife. Bud knows the times have changed since he retired in 1996. Now computers, cell phones, GPSs, drones, DNA testing, and other electric devices are used daily to help catch and convict poachers. Maybe Bud's ideas, arrests, methods, and techniques left enough of a trail for others to follow. Always keep your finger off the trigger until a target is acquired. The refrigerator you save might be your own!

Bud traveled a long way from where he was born. Where he'll end up, nobody knows. He climbed a mountain or two just to see what was on the other side. He rafted some mighty rivers and cast a line to catch the fish therein. He heard the call of the sandhill crane and the wild geese too and heard the whistle of their wings as they flew in the night. Bud has heard the bugle of the elk looking for a fight and has challenged a turkey or two to a midmorning duel.

There is a favorite song of his, "When I Die I May Not Go to Heaven," 'cause he doesn't know if they let cowboys in. If they don't, just let him go to Lester because that was about as close as he'd been to heaven. Bud has instructed his family to spread his ashes over Lester, north of Mount Rainier, when he dies. And some day when you look up into the sky and get a piece of grit in your eye, just think it might be Bud dropping in to say hi.